SCARRED

SCARRED

*A Memoir of
a Childhood Stolen
and a Life Reclaimed*

Clark Fredericks

ATRIA BOOKS

New York   Amsterdam/Antwerp   London   Toronto
Sydney/Melbourne   New Delhi

ATRIA
BOOKS

An Imprint of Simon & Schuster, LLC
1230 Avenue of the Americas
New York, NY 10020

First Atria Books hardcover edition July 2025

ATRIA BOOKS and colophon are trademarks of Simon & Schuster, LLC

Simon & Schuster strongly believes in freedom of expression and stands against
censorship in all its forms. For more information, visit BooksBelong.com.

For information about special discounts for bulk purchases, please contact
Simon & Schuster Special Sales at 1-866-506-1949 or
business@simonandschuster.com.

The Simon & Schuster Speakers Bureau can bring authors to your live
event. For more information or to book an event, contact the Simon &
Schuster Speakers Bureau at 1-866-248-3049 or visit our website at
www.simonspeakers.com.

Interior design by Jill Putorti

Manufactured in the United States of America

1 3 5 7 9 10 8 6 4 2

Library of Congress Cataloging-in-Publication Data has been applied for.

ISBN 978-1-6680-1865-1
ISBN 978-1-6680-1867-5 (ebook)

To my brother, Jay Fredericks, and my childhood neighbor, Jeff Hall, who went to their graves before they had a chance to heal. And to every other victim whose light was dimmed way too early. Your deaths have given me the strength and courage to help others avoid a similar path.

CONTENTS

SCARRED

PROLOGUE

The night my life hit bottom I went to bed after midnight a physical and emotional mess. My left hand, which had been gushing blood earlier, was by now crudely wrapped in paper towels and duct tape. I badly needed a hospital emergency room, but that would mean lots of questions, dangerous questions, starting with *How did this happen?* Sure, I could call it an accident, but who would believe that? *What! You accidentally drove a hunting knife through your own left hand? No. Who did this to you? Let's call the police.*

No! I would have to insist. *No police.*

I felt nothing but dread and torment. I wished to be dead— if only I could avoid dying to get there. My temporary escape was in lines of cocaine chased with cocktails of Xanax and Ketel One vodka. I said goodbye to a couple of visiting friends, left my distraught eighty-one-year-old mother alone to clean up after my bloody homecoming, and finally shut my eyes to whatever was waiting for me out there in the deepest darkness I had ever known.

This was the second-worst day in all my forty-six years. I had just murdered Dennis Pegg, a longtime family friend, my boyhood hero. I killed him without mercy—face-to-face, up close and personal—with my bare hands and a razor-sharp knife, the same knife he taught me how to sharpen when I was just a kid.

Dennis Pegg was a lot of things to a lot of people in my rural hometown of Stillwater, New Jersey. Besides having served as a Boy Scout leader and helping with Cub Scouts, he was a retired sheriff's lieutenant who used to supervise the Sussex County jail. He stayed active in law enforcement, doing weapons-proficiency training for local police officers. He was chaplain of the local American Legion post and vice president of the county birdwatching club; served as a nature guide; and, as a friend of many families, he was widely known for teaching area boys to fish, hunt, and drive a stick shift.

He was also a serial pedophile. Over the years he molested scores of kids. I was one of them. Dennis Pegg raped me when I was twelve years old. At the time, I had no idea there were other victims. I thought it was my fault. I kept my rape a secret bottled up inside me through adolescence into adulthood—a secret I kept from my parents, best friends, and girlfriends. I told no one until that very night when decades of rage finally exploded and left me drenched in the blood of my rapist.

By that night, I was already an alcoholic, a drug addict, a compulsive gambler, and a hopeless loser at love and life. I couldn't hold a decent job. I couldn't maintain a romantic commitment.

I partied like a madman running for his life—probably because that's exactly what I was doing, running for my life. Until that moment I finally snapped.

And as I drifted off to sleep, trapped in a new nightmare, feeling somewhere between homicidal and suicidal, my future seemed almost certainly limited to a cell in some New Jersey state penitentiary. No wonder, then, that my sincerest hope that night was never to wake up again.

Spoiler alert: I did wake up. And I did see the inside of a state prison cell. But I'm telling my story now as a free man—free of prisons real and imagined, and free of the crippling addictions that never let me escape my past.

It is still a tale of horror about a kid terrorized by a trusted friend and abuser. But time has also made it a tale of redemption and recovery—and a true love story about friends and family and second chances.

Part I

THE HOLE
IN MY HEART

I guess you could say I started out flawed. My heart had a hole in it the day I was born. Even the routine childhood illnesses I would face in the years that followed were potentially life-threatening. And it seemed I was always sick. Simple colds turned into bronchitis or pneumonia and made my parents especially nervous because *What about that hole in his heart?* So, as the youngest of three kids, I was the coddled little brother. I was special—*special* as in *fragile*. While most of my pals enjoyed all manner of roughhousing—running, jumping, pushing, and shoving— I had to be protected. They could have fun. I had to be careful. Meanwhile, doctors were afraid to operate on my heart until I got bigger and stronger and healthier. Then, one day those options narrowed. They discovered the hole was now the size of a half-dollar. And it was growing.

Chapter One

THE SCAR

I f only I'd gotten a quarter for every doctor visit in my childhood. Besides my cardiac doctors, there was that emergency
room run in the back seat of my mother's Studebaker after *four-
year-old me* sampled a patch of poisonous mushrooms. I must
have been sedated since I don't remember the stomach pump.
And there were all those other ER visits, beginning before I even
learned how to count, for high fevers mostly, as well as a couple
of five-day hospital admissions for pneumonia. These were my
early years. I still hadn't lost my first baby tooth, but I was getting to know the staff at Newton Medical Center.

Of course, the monster of all medical procedures facing anyone—from *six-year-old me* to someone ten times my age—would
have to be open-heart surgery. Imagine my kid's mind processing how they intended to crack me open and stick needles in my
heart. Scary. No one in my house ever joked about it. Mom and
Dad took it so seriously that we moved to Naples, Florida, for the

two months before surgery. The twin motivations were to soak up lots of winter sunshine and to avoid snotty-nosed little kids with germs to contaminate me. We returned home to rural New Jersey just long enough to pack for another month in a New York City hospital.

We had booked an April surgery date at the venerable Mount Sinai Hospital in upper Manhattan. Mom and Dad were already unnerved enough getting me admitted to the hospital, but that same day they were victims of a crime. Our family car, parked on a street near the hospital, was broken into—a window smashed and Mom's suitcase swiped. It had all the clothes and accessories she needed for a month's residency at my bedside. An NYPD precinct house came to her rescue, raising donations to fund a replacement wardrobe and slippers.

My first several days in the pediatric ward of Mount Sinai were more fun than I expected. There were so many other kids. My favorite was Collette. She was seven, an older woman. The nurses let us play with the wheelchairs. We ended up racing each other up and down the halls and around the nurses' station. Between all the pre- and postsurgical testing that kids in our ward were always getting, we also got to watch creature feature movies at night. Collette liked *The Thing*. I liked *Creature from the Black Lagoon*.

Dr. Feldman, my surgeon, wasn't so much fun, though he seemed like a nice man. His explanation of the upcoming procedure was always calm, matter-of-fact, and clinical. I'm sure it was intended mostly to reassure my mother. But *six-year-old me* processed more alarming images: of grown men and women in white scrubs cutting open my chest, finding a heart full of holes, attacking it with needles and thread, blood spraying everywhere. I was so terrified on the eve of surgery that I begged my mother, who would be bunking in my room, "Please, sleep with your eyes open!"

Surgery turned out to be the easy part. I slept through it. But the recovery was one ordeal after another. For one thing, I was thirsty coming out of the anesthetic. But I wasn't allowed to drink any liquid for what seemed like hours. My body was getting what it needed through an IV hookup. Severe dry mouth was a separate misery. My only option was to suck on moist Q-tips dipped in lemon juice.

A serious risk to my recovery was mucus buildup in my lungs. Prevention efforts began almost immediately with chest-racking coughs—coughs on demand, doctors' orders. I had to cough up the phlegm. It was a matter of life or death—or at least the only way to avoid sending suction tubes down my nose and into my lungs. I had to cough constantly—and *strenuously*—even if it hurt. And it hurt like crazy.

I quickly realized that Mom was feeling my every cringe of pain. So I tried not to show it, but every wince of agony I couldn't hide made her feel worse than I did. We were a mess. Still I kept trying to cough, out of fear I might suffocate in my own mucus— or as the *six-year-old me* understood it, I might drown in my own snot.

You can only imagine how bad it had to get for me finally to give up and submit to having my lungs pumped out. I didn't sleep through that one. And that was nowhere near the end of our torture.

When it came time to change my surgical dressing and re- move my stitches, I yelped like an injured puppy. The pulling out of those first sutures from my sensitive incision caused an unexpected burning pain. The second stitch hurt worse than the first. And I must've had a million of them. Again, I cried out in desperation and begged my mother, "Please, Mom! Make them stop. No more. No more."

Having survived surgery, the coughing regimen, and suture removal, I was most bothered by the prominent scar form- ing along the incision on my chest. It was more than a simple straight line. It was a big, ugly welt of a scar—as if I'd had a zip- per installed down my sternum. Somewhere in my DNA was a gene that made me prone to somewhat disfiguring keloid scar- ring. Any potential career as a male swimsuit model I might have ever wished for was over.

To my parents' credit, they tried to make me less self-conscious about the oh-so-prominent blemish by treating it like a souvenir from New York, not an embarrassment; made the scar the star of a family party game, instead of keeping it a secret.

"Hey, Clarkie—come over here and show Mrs. Smith your zipper!"

That was a signal for me to stop whatever I was doing, stand before my parents and their friends, and dutifully lift my shirt up to my chin. According to house rules, each gawker had to pay me a quarter. Sometimes, I felt a bit like a freak, but it gave my parents the chance to rave about me, so I humored them.

I was their "golden boy." I was the brave little guy that sur- vived a life-and-death ordeal. They marveled aloud at how strong

I'd been. They wanted to show me off to friends. Inevitably, the show produced oohs and aahs and laughs and words of praise. I think Jay and Holly were getting sick of all the attention focused on their little brother. But, then, so was I.

My scar made me feel different from other kids. My parents may have tried to ward off my insecurity with their praise, but I was only growing *more* self-conscious, not less. Still, I continued to pull up my shirt on request. My proud mom and dad seemed to be getting such a kick out of it, I didn't have the heart to complain.

Besides, it was my primary source of quarters.

One afternoon that summer I took a break from play in our backyard to pour myself a glass of iced tea in the kitchen. Then I plopped down in the den to watch some TV cartoons. That's when I heard the creak of our front door opening. People didn't lock front doors in Stillwater, New Jersey, then, or now.

A familiar voice called out, "Hello, anybody home?"

I jumped up. It was Dennis Pegg.

"Hey, little buddy—where's everybody?" he boomed.

I pointed him to the backyard, but Pegg suggested we just "sit down and spend a few minutes together."

Dennis was a family friend. He was also a Boy Scout leader who wore a badge and packed a gun as a Sussex County sheriff's officer. He was a big kid himself, a gregarious outdoorsman who loved to hunt and fish and teach neighborhood boys how to gut fish and keep our hunting knives razor-sharp. He was more than six feet tall and weighed at least 250 pounds—a giant in my eyes, a living, breathing, enthusiastic action figure, a local hero, and an overgrown pal.

During hunting season, Dennis sometimes stalked deer in the wooded portion of my family's adjacent twenty-acre property. Once, he even lived in our basement while recuperating from a serious traffic accident. Mom had offered to feed him and do his laundry until he recovered enough to take care of himself. He ate at our dinner table for a couple of weeks. He became "family."

On this summer afternoon Dennis was out of uniform, dressed in cargo shorts and a polo shirt that accentuated his powerful physique. He sat on the couch and patted the cushion next to him, an unspoken invitation for me to take a seat beside him. I hopped right up.

"I've got a quarter for you. Can I see your zipper again?"

"Sure," I said without hesitation.

Dennis had often asked to see my scar. It was, I figured, his way of justifying gifts of a quarter or two. So, of course, I lifted my shirt. He studied my scar, maybe a bit more intently this time. Maybe because this was his first private viewing. I was ready to end it and pocket my twenty-five cents when Dennis asked me to wait.

"How about I give you a dollar. Just let me see what it feels like."

"Sure," I said again.

Dennis leaned closer and, holding three of his meaty fingers tightly together, found the top of my scar. His touch followed the ridge of scar tissue slowly down my chest to the bottom of the zipper. Gently, he rubbed the rough edges back up toward my collarbone, then followed the scar back down again.

This time his fingers continued beyond the scar's edges. He was feeling the bare skin of my belly and abdomen. This time his three-finger touch explored along my belt line, pressing and probing.

"Are you still sore? Is your stomach tender from the operation?"

"Not at all." I lowered my shirt.

Dennis gave me four quarters and asked me, "You and I are buddies, right?"

I nodded with a shrug.

"You can't tell anyone that I gave you a dollar, okay? Or that I touched your scar. That will be our little secret, okay?"

"Okay, Dennis." I was puzzled. He had never said anything like that before.

"Are you sure you can keep a secret?" he pressed me. "Because if you can't, it will ruin our friendship."

I was hurt that he would question my loyalty, that my friend might not trust me. "No, I won't tell anyone. I can keep a secret."

Dennis smiled and told me to go put those quarters in my piggy bank. He was heading outside "to say hi to your mom and dad." I rushed off to make my dollar deposit before settling back on the couch, alone with my iced tea and another episode of *Scooby-Doo*.

Chapter Two

WORTHLESS
LITTLE THINGS

Sussex County, in the northwest corner of New Jersey, was a great place to be a kid. It had state parks, state forests, and wildlife management areas. It even included a stretch of the Appalachian Trail. For nearly a century our backyards were the summer destination for city people looking for all manner of outdoor recreation—swimming, sailing, fishing, hunting, hiking, and horseback riding. Yet, it was barely an hour's drive from the heart of Manhattan.

For us local kids, it was a year-round adventure land, our very own kingdom of secret fishing holes, magical woods, and private trails. Once we mastered riding bikes, we could hit the road from morning to dusk with only minimal parental supervision. *Just be home before dinner.* We knew the drill.

Of course, there were other rules, too. Such as *Never hop in a car with strangers.* Or *Never go home with a stranger.* And simply *Never trust a stranger.* But, so far as I can recall, no one ever warned us to beware of friends.

I lived a quick bike ride from the dam at Paulinskill Lake. It was a leafy setting near well-equipped playgrounds with soccer fields and basketball courts and good fishing from the lakeshore or downstream. Dennis Pegg was a regular around the lake, too, always happy to teach us the ways of nature and where and what to fish. He told us to call him Denny.

The lake was great for three kinds of trout—rainbow, brown, and brook—a couple kinds of bass, American shad, and bluegill. All good eating. But it swarmed with sunfish. Denny didn't like them. By that, I mean he didn't like them even existing in our fishing waters. Me and the guys called them sunnies. Denny called the fish "stupid," "gullible," "worthless little things." They were too easy to catch and not good to eat.

It was true. The sunfish would strike any shiny hook. No bait required. My pals and I just tossed them back—catch and release, we called it. At least we were catching something. Denny made a point to smash his sunfish catches against the rocks.

That was the summer after I turned eight, my first summer as a Cub Scout. One day a group of neighbor boys and I were fishing downstream from the dam under an old one-lane wooden bridge when Dennis stopped his pickup truck just above us. He jumped out to send us on a mission.

"Hey, I want you boys to catch as many sunnies as you can," he called down, saying he would be back in fifteen minutes. We didn't ask questions. We knew what Denny thought of the lowly sunfish, but if he wanted sunnies, we'd get him lots of sunnies.

Me and Roy and Jonathan and Shawn—all fellow Cub Scouts, classmates, and neighbors—pulled out our nets and plunged into the stream. We had filled a bucket with a flopping bunch by the time Dennis returned. He stopped his pickup truck again on the one-lane and summoned us. "Bring 'em up here."

He told us to lay out our flopping catch along the tire marks of the single lane. And just like good little soldiers, we did as he said. Then we stood back. That's when Denny seemed taken over by some kind of dark mood. The fun-loving guy went grim, his jaw tightened. It was like his whole persona changed. He was suddenly *Mean Denny.*

He put his pickup in gear and slowly rolled ahead, driving across the lineup of fish, then backing up and doing it again, crushing them into mush—their eyeballs popped out, their guts squirted under the wheels of a half-ton truck, all while Dennis repeatedly bellowed out the two lessons he wanted us all to remember:

"Sunnies are worthless. And this is what you do with worthless things."

The four of us were then told to pick up the mangled fish remains and toss them back down into the stream like so much garbage. I don't remember any of us having much to say as we cleaned up.

It was a message any eight-year-old could understand. I sure didn't want Denny to think I was worthless.

And there was one more thing, he insisted, glaring at us: "This stays between us. This is our secret."

We nodded in unison.

Chapter Three

MORE SECRETS

The next summer, after I turned nine, Denny took me under his wing, offering more personalized fishing lessons. It meant we spent more time together in his pickup truck, too, talking about fish but also grown-up things—like his job at the jail, his old-furniture collection, his travels to Wyoming and Montana, and how to tie knots. The knots were just to help me get into the Boy Scouts, once I was old enough. But whatever it was that we talked about, simply bonding with an adult was heady stuff to me. He even started sharing beers with me.

"You know," he said in a confidential tone one afternoon as he opened another pop-top can of Budweiser, "I could get into a lot of trouble down at the jail if you told anyone I gave you these beers." He handed me a second round from his six-pack.

Of course, in my slightly inebriated nine-year-old mind, I was asking myself, *Hey, why would I ever do that? Why would I*

ruin this? I'm having beers and hearing jokes and inside-the-jail
stories with this great guy. How many kids get to do this?

But, then, some of his secrets edged just a bit closer to forbid-
den territory. Denny said he had come into possession of a stash
of photos through some complicated chain of events—a friend
had bought an old farmhouse that had an old desk that had a
drawer full of racy Polaroid pictures. He seemed eager to share
them, saying, "You wanna see some naked pictures?"

Again, we were just a couple of guys having beers in the cab
of a pickup truck. Now we would be drinking Buds and talking fish and furniture and going through pictures of naked girls.
What could be wrong with that?

But this desk held a photographic treasure of Polaroid origi-
nals that turned out to be exclusively close-ups of prepubescent
genitalia. The *nine-year-old me* didn't know what to make of
penis pictures, or what it was that Denny found so amusing about
boys' penises as he laughed and joked his way through the photos,
tossing them one by one in my lap with "Oh, look at this one."

In those days, if anyone had suspected that our idyllic outdoor
wonderland might include a child-trolling pedophile, that notion was not widely shared. Yet, there were early warnings about
Dennis Pegg. One came that very same summer, from a six-year-
old eyewitness named Kathy. I didn't know her then. Neither did
I know back then what a pedophile was. Kathy would tell me her
story decades later, the same story she'd told only a few adults
when she was six—and scared.

The little girl had just arrived at a local farm where her family boarded their horses. It was a great day for horseback riding,

and she was especially eager to get saddled up. A group of older girls, some as old as fifth and sixth graders, had invited her to join them. She rushed to the tack room for her riding gear only to barge in on what was for her a confusing scene.

She said she saw Dennis Pegg and a boy of about eleven kissing passionately. It was immediately obvious to the child that her sudden arrival was most unwelcome.

"Get the fuck outta here," an angry Pegg shouted at her once, then twice, before adding, "And don't you go telling anyone, either."

Kathy had frozen, torn between flight and pressing on to grab her riding gear, but the big, raging adult was too intimidating. She raced out seeking the protection of an adult friend who had driven her to the stables. The friend summoned the stables' owner, and a barn-side confrontation put Pegg on the defensive.

He said the boy was his nephew. He accused Kathy of making up a wild story. Pegg finally exploded, "Are you going to believe me or this lying little bitch?"

The owner elected to evict Pegg, his "nephew," and the horse that Pegg had been boarding at the farm.

For a child who had never been the target of such anger or profanity, the incident remained a troubling secret (until she told me about it, as an adult). In the summer of '72, the traumatized six-year-old never told anyone else, not even her parents.

I was keeping secrets from my parents, too—about sneaking beers with Denny, about those dirty pictures, and about all the little lies he and I shared, lies that seemed so harmless at the time. I just felt special hanging with Denny and playing grown-up. I couldn't possibly know that I was being groomed by what the New Jersey State Police would describe, years later, as a masterful pedophile, "a professional hunter of children."

Had there existed such a thing as a playbook for pedophilia, Dennis Pegg could probably have written it. He was meticulous and patient and knew how to foster the trust of kids and their parents. And he used the Cub Scouts as a farm team for his Boy Scout recruits—maintaining a pipeline of underage kids at various stages, from early grooming to primed for molestation.

That summer, just before I would start fourth grade, Denny was getting me ready for the next stage.

Chapter Four

THE GIFT

I saw none of that coming. Riding with Denny in his pickup was almost always a friendly experience. He would tell stories and make jokes, reach over to accentuate a punch line with a pat on the knee or thigh or sometimes higher (accidentally, I always thought). He had more extensive contact in mind with the *ten-year-old me*. He insisted on giving me instruction in the ancient sport of wrestling.

The competitive version played in schools and at the Olympics is a demanding test of strength and agility. But Dennis Pegg's version was all about hand-to-hand combat. Lots of hands, as in grappling, grabbing, and groping.

Dennis assured me that he had often wrestled with my older brother, Jay, and our friend Jeff. "Let's see what you've got," he challenged me. Of course, this was bound to be a one-sided contest. Denny was four or five times my size; he outweighed me by close to two hundred pounds. He was the mountain. I was the molehill.

But he kept encouraging me, telling me how much fun Jay and Jeff had had when they wrestled and partied with him. "Yeah." He laughed, enjoying those memories. "They used to get so drunk afterward that I had to take their clothes off and put them to bed." He had pictures, he told me.

Our first physical workout on the floor of his living room was preceded by a couple of Budweisers. "C'mon, show me what you've got," he exhorted again, kneeling in front of me and inviting an attack.

I charged him, throwing every ounce of my fifty-some pounds into him, knocking him over—or so he feigned. I was on top, trying to pin him. He twisted and turned, flopped and floundered, always staying on the defensive—making no aggressive moves as I panted from the exertion of trying to budge the big man. I began to sweat. He was letting me climb all over his supine body, fighting me off ever so gently. Until abruptly his mood changed. He went dark, sort of angry it seemed. He turned physically rough with me.

Suddenly, I was the one on the bottom—pinned down by his crushing weight, unable to move in any direction, unable to push myself up off the floor. He began gyrating and rubbing against me. He growled at me to resist, to fight harder. I couldn't move, but he was impatient, sharply ordering me, "C'mon, you can get out. C'mon! Squirm!"

Things went no further that first day. But it turned out to be the beginning of more aggressive, full-body touching. Denny kept finding excuses to have me come over to his home, have a beer, get comfortable, and then wrestle. Of course, I almost always wound up on the bottom.

The next summer my visits to Denny's house sometimes coincided with Cub Scout work. I was especially determined to master my knots, one of those skills necessary to join the big kids in Boy Scouts. It didn't occur to me to question his implication that somehow my fine eye-hand coordination would benefit from chugging down a glass or two of blackberry brandy.

On one of those days, he came out of the bathroom with his cargo shorts looking funny. I couldn't help but laugh; it looked to me as if he'd inserted a stick into his fly, making the front of his shorts stick out. I thought it was a joke. But Denny wasn't laughing. He suggested a game he called "bumping logs."

This would be the *eleven-year-old me*'s introduction to an adult erection.

It wasn't really a suggestion at all. I didn't even get to ask what "bumping logs" was before Denny had lifted me up and was grinding his hips into me, bumping the front of his cargo shorts into my shorts. Then, he said, as if rendering a disappointing diagnosis, "Your log's not ready. We gotta get your log ready." That's when he sat me down on a kitchen chair and told me to close my eyes and keep them closed, "no matter what happens."

He pulled down my shorts. I think I stopped breathing. I'm sure I squinted my eyes even more tightly shut—until he took my penis into his mouth. Then, I was instantly wide-eyed and terrified. *What the hell is going on?* I gripped both arms of the wooden chair as if holding on for dear life. My entire body went rigid. I couldn't breathe. In a flash, all the air had been sucked out of the room. The *eleven-year-old me* was at a total loss to comprehend the what, the why, the where, of what was happening. I hoped he didn't bite me.

At the same time, from what I could see—and what I wished I wasn't seeing—Denny was rubbing his own penis. The moment seemed to last an eternity, before he finally calmed down and released his suction. I still couldn't breathe. I wanted to throw myself in the river and float away. More than anything else, I wanted to forget what had just happened.

But I also knew, *No one will ever know about this.* Somehow, I felt instinctively that the best way to forget about it was to tell no one. No friend, no parent, no one. Not ever.

Denny didn't have to ask this time. He didn't have to threaten. He didn't have to remind me again about how our friendship relied on keeping our little secret. At eleven I already knew that I wouldn't be sharing this with anyone. I was fully prepared to take this secret to my grave.

I continued to see Dennis around town and down by the dam and recreation area through the summer into fall. This was Denny's playground, too. My friends, classmates, and fellow Scouts were his friends, his Scout troops. I would learn only later that they were his molestation targets, too. Back then, however, it never occurred to me that other kids in my town might also be harboring their own Denny secrets.

I started sixth grade in the fall and turned twelve in November. The next time I spent any time with Dennis was Christmas Day at my house. Over the years, he had been a regular visitor during the holidays. I felt no discomfort in his presence. Surrounded as I was by my family, it was easy to leave the past summer's bumping-log incident buried deep in my psyche.

As usual for such occasions, Dennis arrived with presents for me and everyone else. My gift was a knife-sharpening kit. And as usual at Christmastime, the Fredericks family's famous eggnog was in plentiful supply. This season, Dad had made me the house bartender—letting me mix the eggnog with his recipe of equal and generous parts rum, sherry, and oak-fermented brandy.

On arrival, Denny greeted me cheerfully, as always, and grinned. "Give me an eggnog and I'll show you how to sharpen that hunting knife of yours."

Then, fueled with that high-octane eggnog, he played Santa, teaching me how to slide a blade ever-so-carefully over an oiled whetstone, striving for a perfect eighteen-degree blade angle: bringing the knife down and then back, turned to one side, then the other, again and again and again, honing an edge fine enough to slice with precision the flesh of any animal.

Chapter Five

THE DOG CRIED

After Christmas, Denny approached me about doing him a favor while also accomplishing a good deed for our community. As a Cub Scout in need of good deeds, I was open to hearing more. It turned out to be, at least on the surface, a plan to teach one of Denny's supposedly careless hunting buddies to be more cautious in the woods. The guy had a tendency, Denny said, to shoot first and make sure no other hunters were endangered later.

"I'm afraid someone's going to get hurt," he told me in the gravest of tones. "He's always shooting from the hip. He sees something, and he instantly fires away at it. There's no awareness of his surroundings. I'm just afraid he's going to hurt someone."

That's why Denny said he needed my help. "We can teach him a lesson."

Cockamamie doesn't begin to describe the plan Denny laid out. It would require me to pose as an accidental gunshot victim, lying in the brush out in the woods, slathered in fake blood and gasping for my last breath. What exactly would happen once the ruse was played out? Was I meant to jump up and say, "Surprise!"? That was never addressed. And besides, I wasn't there to ask questions. I was a prop.

Besides, who was I, least of all that *twelve-year-old me*, to question a professional firearms instructor and local authority on gun safety. This was Dennis Pegg's world, and I was just a kid occupying it.

Even to a preteen me, it sounded like a joke. Who could possibly design a scheme like this, no less fall for it? But Denny was dead serious. I knew it because he reminded me more than once that this was to be just between us. "Don't you go telling your parents about it."

He also insisted that I practice. "I want you gurgling," he said, demanding a death rattle that I could never manage. He told me to keep working on it. He coached me on shallow breathing and heavy breathing. He would press one of his big, meaty hands against my stomach to see, he said, how much it was moving, or not moving. I wasn't good at acting the victim, and Denny got impatient. But he never seemed discouraged. He knew this was going to work.

One day while I was out riding my ten-speed, Denny pulled up and said he wanted to do another session of breathing practice. He tossed my bike into the back of his pickup and said, "Let's go to my house. We'll have a beer and work on your breathing."

His home was the last place I wanted to go. I hadn't been back since the bumping-logs episode the summer before. But still, there I was, in his truck, heading to his house, beating myself up in silence for going this far. It was a short drive, but I already knew I didn't want it to end. My mind was a jumble:

I can't believe this is happening. Why did I even get in the truck? I just want to go home. Please, let him leave me alone. Please, God. Maybe we'll just practice, and then we'll be done. Oh, God help me. What'll I do? How do I get out of this?

His hillside house was isolated from Millbrook Road, set back in a wooded area at the end of a long driveway with a ninety-degree right turn midway up the hill. It was a warm day, but I figured Dennis must have left his heater running inside the house because it was stifling hot.

I immediately drank down a can of Budweiser, welcoming the cool, the wet, and its calming effect on my nerves. He gave me a second can. Then he poured me a glass of blackberry brandy.

"Why don't you take your shirt off and lay on the bed here," he said, choreographing my moves and my sounds. He wanted me to raise and lower my stomach. He reminded me that I was supposed to be having trouble breathing. I was supposed to be in pain. "Nah, nah . . . you're not doing it right," he complained. "Your breathing's not in sync with what you're doing with your stomach muscles."

He wanted a better view of my lower diaphragm, below the belt line of my jeans. A moment later I was on his bed in my underwear. I was by now drenched in sweat from fear and the blazing heat, along with mounting agitation from trying and failing to satisfy Denny's demands. Still, he urged me to keep trying. He complained that I needed to sound more in distress. Maybe if we could drive more air out of my gut, put more pressure on my abdomen, maybe that would help make my gasps more convincing.

He had an idea. "I'm going to get on the bed and scissor you." It was a wrestling move. He locked me in a viselike grip between his massive thighs. I couldn't breathe. I couldn't move. I was in the man's complete physical control.

For the next eternity, I was his rag doll. He was behind me. He was on top of me. I was in pain. I was screaming. I was sobbing. I was pleading. I wanted my very existence to cease.

I'd never felt so utterly alone. Suddenly, I had no family, no one on the planet who loved me. Even God was dead, despite all my years of faithful service as an Episcopal altar boy. Indeed, the first sparks of a fierce anger were only beginning. *How bad can I possibly have been to deserve this? Where the hell is He in my hour of terror and torment?*

Finally, I collapsed exhausted—naked and used and crushed—feeling as stupid and worthless as those gullible sunnies. But even at the deepest depths of my suffering, I had become vaguely aware of another sound—a long, mournful, incessant howl that matched my screams, moment for moment.

It was Pegg's hunting dog, a lovable big brown hound of mixed pedigree tied up just outside. While I sobbed through my rape, the dog cried, too.

We cleaned up and Pegg offered an apology of sorts. "Listen, what happened was an accident. We were all sweaty. I just slipped in."

Then he invited the dog into the house and brought the hound over to me, holding him by the collar. Before I could reach out to pet him, Pegg reared back with his right hand and began pounding the defenseless animal with his fist. He hammered the dog again and again and again, ignoring my screams and wails and pleas for him to stop.

The lovable hound yipped, yelped, and whimpered, then relented. His eyes rolled back and he fell to the floor, motionless at my feet. I was by then in a frenzy, sobbing out of control. Pegg insisted that I listen to him.

"You see that dog? You keep your mouth shut or that's what will happen to you. Are you listening to me?"

The *twelve-year-old me* gave him the nod he demanded. But the *twelve-year-old me* was now unsure what was worse: the rape or the brutal beating of the dog that cried. And at that very moment, I blamed myself for absolutely *every bad thing* that had just happened—on what I already knew would be, forever and always, the worst day of my life.

Part II

THE HOLE IN MY SOUL

He dropped me off back by the lake after the rape. But I was desperate to avoid seeing any of my friends. I had to get away from the dam, so I ditched my ten-speed in the weeds and took off running down the river. I found a place completely alone where I sat and rocked back and forth, my arms wrapped around me. My mind was already telling me, right there at that moment, *We are never gonna talk about this. Talking about it means reliving it, and that's never gonna happen. Ever.* And that's how it went. The *little-boy me* never said a thing. Neither did the *teenager me*, or the *young-man me*. It would stay completely locked up inside me for the next thirty years. But a secret born of fear, shame, and guilt also came with caustic side effects that began burning a hole in my soul. And like that hole in my heart, it grew.

Chapter Six

BREAKING AWAY

I wanted never to see Dennis Pegg again for the rest of my life. But for the next couple of days, I woke up every morning in a cold sweat with him on my mind. Was he going to show up somewhere and remind me that we still had a fake shooting accident to pull off? Half of me argued to forget it, that the whole story must have been concocted to get me into his house to do what he did to me. But the other half was freaking out that this whack job might still try to use me for that crazy plot.

I was talking to myself: *I gotta get out of this. I can't, I just can't let him use me again.* But I couldn't think straight, either. Finally, I got up the courage to approach my father. Not about the rape. I just felt I needed him to forbid my involvement in that harebrained "hunting lesson."

"Well, you know, Dennis," I started to explain. "He's got this hunting friend who shoots from the hip." I launched into details of Pegg's scenario. I didn't get far before Dad exploded.

"What!? Is Dennis out of his mind? Absolutely not! I can't believe what you're telling me. You're not gonna lie out in the woods pretending to be shot!" Dad started for the telephone. "I'm going to call him right now and tell him you're not doing that."

I hadn't seen it coming. Now, with terrible visions of mushed sunfish and a battered dog dancing in my head, I pleaded, "No, please. Dad, please don't call him! I beg of you. Please. It was just an idea he had. Don't make a big deal. I'll tell him myself. Please! Let me do it. I'll tell him you said 'absolutely not,' okay?"

Dad relented, but now it meant I actually had to face Pegg again. So after days of avoiding the playgrounds around the dam, I returned with feelings of panic and dread. I knew I would see him there. If that's where kids were, that's where Pegg was. And it didn't take long. He pulled up next to me in his truck, rolled down his window, and called out a friendly "Hey, buddy, how you doing?"

I had rehearsed a cool, low-key conversation in my mind, but face-to-face, with him sitting at the wheel of his truck, I pretty much just blurted it out: "Hey, I told my dad something about your plan, that we were gonna fake getting me shot to scare your friend, and he said, 'Absolutely not.'"

Suddenly, I was looking at *Mean Denny*. He went absolutely ballistic. His face flushed red. He scowled, his lips curled, his jaw tightened. He started screaming curse words as he pounded his steering wheel, using the same fist that had beat the dog.

"You fucking little asshole. I told you, I fucking warned you what would happen if you opened up your mouth!"

I quickly assured him, "I didn't say anything else, Dennis. I just talked about the hunting thing. That's all. I promise."

But Dennis kept beating his steering wheel and repeating, as if in rhythm, "I fucking told you. I fucking warned you. I fucking told you. I fucking . . ."

Had there been some cosmic stopwatch measuring the span of my relationship with Dennis Pegg, it would have stopped at that moment. When he roared off still raging, I felt only relief. Pegg no longer controlled me. As brief and tentative as that last confrontation turned out to be, it represented a big win for the *twelve-year-old me.* I'd done it. I stood up to the Devil.

Soon after that I dropped out of the Scout program. I explained to my mom that scouting was now just "too dorky" for someone my age. My days hanging around the dam, Pegg's hunting grounds, ended then, too. I traded my ten-speed for a motorized dirt bike so I could ride with older boys farther from home. It was they who introduced me to weed.

I thought I was growing up. Mostly, though, I was acting out, doing little things that future therapists would see as familiar conduct among child sex abuse victims—playing with matches (and nearly lighting fire to our house), shoplifting cigars at the CVS (and getting caught in the act).

But those sexual abuse secrets? They remained buried in my soul.

Chapter Seven

HE NEVER TOUCHED ME

M y father's patience with the new *weed-smoking me* finally reached its breaking point when he found my stash. He left the contraband prominently displayed on my bed. By the time I got home from school that day, he had also researched the availability of military schools in the tristate area. He made it clear: I could either knock off the dope smoking or I'd have to get used to uniforms and reveille every morning. I lied and secretly picked a third option: to be more discreet about my drug use.

Dad's ultimatum only hardened my resolve to keep my silence about Dennis. It certainly was no invitation to open up about the abuse tormenting the troubled kid that I was clearly becoming.

Subconsciously, as I've been told many times since then and in countless hours of therapy, I was already crying out for help. All that self-destructive behavior—from junior pyromaniac to amateur shoplifter to boozing-doping adolescent—turned out to be predictable to experts on child sexual abuse victims.

And then there was that seventh-grade English short-story writing assignment that no one, least of all me, noticed was another distress signal. Even its title, "Being a Slave," captured the underlying sense of helplessness I carried in those days. In this homework project, the *real me* wrote about a *fictional me*, one who had repelled an attempted rape. In the story, we were fellow slaves on a slave ship, me and my attacker. I was a trusting character, but one who ended up wielding a steel bar as a weapon to hold him off. At least in fiction, I was able to fight back. In fiction, I saved myself.

My dreams drew from the same material, even if they enacted the scene differently. That was a place where I waited for some Superman figure to appear in time to rescue me from Dennis Pegg. But I always woke up still his victim.

When we got our graded papers back in class, the *real me* was rewarded with an A on "Being a Slave." My teacher never asked about the dark implications of the paper, or why a thirteen-year-old boy was writing about rape. Her only comment was about the story's structure. Use more paragraphs to break it up, she advised.

My secrets continued to protect Pegg, and as I would later learn, he used his impunity to actively troll boys and young men throughout our corner of Sussex County. He was promoted to supervising sergeant at the county jail in Newton, where he volunteered to mentor young inmates. Some of them—released from custody, and with nowhere to go and little cash—he invited to stay in his spare bedroom. It was all done very much in the open. Pegg waited in the jail parking lot to drive them to his house.

I came home from school one afternoon and found my dad in the kitchen. "I want to talk with you, Son," he said. We sat down together at the table.

"I've heard something disturbing about Dennis Pegg. There are rumors going around town. People have been picking up young hitchhikers, especially late at night. Different guys who said the same thing—that they had just got out of Newton jail, that Pegg had offered them a place to stay, but that in the middle of the night they'd wake up to Pegg crawling into their bed. Then they'd freak out and run."

I knew where this was going. By this time, I was probably a high school freshman, maybe fourteen. Even my secret was getting old. But I had never been asked a direct question about it. My dilemma was what to say. Should I grab the opportunity to tell all, to get it off my chest? I tried not to remember my helplessness under the big man's weight or my terror as he beat the dog that crumpled at my feet. Would I feel better if the people I loved knew what a terrible thing I'd gone through all alone and scared?

Dad finally asked, "Clark, did Dennis Pegg ever touch you?"

I didn't hesitate, I lied immediately. "No, Dad, he never touched me."

———————

That was the first time I heard that anyone was talking about Pegg molesting people, like it was public knowledge or something. I had already suspected that other friends and fellow Scouts might have been targeted or molested. I wondered about my older brother, Jay, and our neighbor Jeff. I had never asked them about it, but Pegg told me he had wrestled them both, too. I knew what "wrestling" meant in Pegg's world.

Michael Funari was another fishing pal, classmate, and fellow Scout. I didn't know it at the time, but Mike had gotten a summer job mowing the grass around Pegg's house. Comparing notes years later, he told me a familiar story—that Pegg plied him with alcohol, then showed him pornographic photos before sexually molesting him in the same house where I had been raped.

Mike did what I couldn't. He told his mom what Pegg did. Mary Ann Funari took her son down to the New Jersey State Police barracks in Newton, where Mike was interviewed. He and his mom filed a formal complaint accusing Pegg of sexually assaulting a minor.

Mary Ann Funari was a familiar figure around Newton. She worked for years at the local Dunkin' Donuts, a favorite of cops and kids, just across the street from state police headquarters. She was working the late shift when Pegg learned about the potential career-ending criminal complaint against him. He went straight into attack mode.

Pegg began lurking around the doughnut shop at all hours. He made threatening calls to Mike at his home, sometimes telling him he knew when the boy's mother was alone at the store, when she took her smoke breaks out back, then repeating ominously that anything could happen to her.

A few days later Mike returned to police headquarters and withdrew his complaint. There's no evidence that any attempt had been made to investigate the allegations. No investigators ever followed up with the Funari family. And no record of the complaint exists today. Back then, in the early 1980s, it would have been subject to a strict five-year statute of limitations.

Some weeks after Mike Funari had privately withdrawn his unpublicized complaint, Dad called me to my bedroom for another private conversation. I sat on the end of my bed as he explained, "I just had coffee with Mary Ann Funari. She said Dennis Pegg raped her boy."

I tried to act surprised.

Dad said he had a question to ask me. "Before you answer, I want you to know, you will never have to testify. You will never have to answer another question. I will take care of Dennis Pegg myself. You understand?"

What the hell? My dad's gonna take care of Pegg? What does that even mean? Dad's gonna kill that sonuvabitch? Dad's gonna go to prison? It'll be my fault! It's all my fault.

I was surprised at how easy it was for me to act surprised—especially since I doubted that anything involving the dark side of Pegg could ever surprise me. Dad told me the Funaris had dropped the official charges after Pegg threatened them. I fought back a terrible urge to vent, keeping it all inside.

OF COURSE he threatened them! That's the same SOB I know. That's the fuckin' asshole that hurts kids and dogs.

"I've gotta ask you again, Son," Dad said at last. "Did that child molester ever touch you?"

"No, Dad," I lied. "He never touched me."

And with that, the matter was dropped.

But I couldn't help noticing that the secrecy protecting Dennis Pegg wasn't holding like it used to. It seemed to be leaking out all over. Around this time, the Sussex County jail made a new hire, bringing aboard a corrections officer named Debby. On her first day she was taken aside by a veteran jail guard who pointed out Sergeant Pegg.

"Listen," said the old jailer. "If you've got children, just watch out for that guy. He likes little boys."

Chapter Eight

YOU BAFFLE ME

O ne problem I found, being an altar boy with a terrible secret, was keeping a straight face when the old minister at
Hope Episcopal Church preached about his version of God. In
sermons and prayers, he would tell us that if we did good, God
would reward us. But if we stepped out of line, we risked the
wrath of God. I had known for a fact since the day I was raped
that it just didn't work that way. When the Devil took me, God
didn't do a damn thing to save me.

Yet, there I was in church most Sunday mornings, wearing
my white acolyte's robe, carrying the cross, and helping the Rev-
erend Father pour the wine, serve communion, and take up the
collection, even as my crisis of faith festered into rage.

I wasn't even old enough yet to drive, but by my early teens I
was already a closet skeptic about all matters spiritual. There was
certainly no sanctuary in prayer. Whenever I bowed my head and
closed my eyes, my brain filled the darkness with vivid memories

of the rape. Those images stopped only when I opened my eyes. So, I stopped praying. And finally, as I had with the Scouts and the old fishing hole down by the dam, I gave up going to church.

I weaseled out of it by pestering Mom not to drag me along. With my dad often away on business trips and both of my adult siblings off on their own, Mom mostly went to church alone. I couldn't think about her. I was miserable—furious at God and everything about Him. I didn't like myself much, either. And that hole in my soul, it just kept growing.

High school turned out to be my launchpad to alcohol excess. In those days, New Jersey was wide open to underage drinking. The state relied on paper driver's licenses that included no ID photos, and no one checked expiration dates. So, if my older brother's license expired when he was twenty, he could hand it down to me, and I could use it as my own. I had easy access to bars and liquor stores as early as age fourteen or fifteen. Then there were keg parties and BYO Yukon Jack and sneaking drinks at school events.

Me and the captains of our school's wrestling, football, and basketball teams got smashed one morning and decided to get back to school in time for afternoon classes. Our blotto states were exposed two minutes later. We were all suspended for a week. My mom, who worked in the school library at the time, chewed me out for being an embarrassment. I suspect I embarrassed her not only for my drunkenness but for stupidly thinking I could get away with it.

Grades had always come easily to me, but under the rising influence of weed, booze, beer, and parties, my academic performance slipped to abject mediocrity. On a school trip to the

Jersey Shore, me and some buddies ditched our classmates to try out my brother's expired driver's license on a liquor store clerk. We were having a great time on the boardwalk when a teacher tapped me on the shoulder and said, "What the hell are you guys doing?" We had to watch while our drinks were poured out, one by one, into a garbage can.

Mr. Garret, our principal, threatened me with banishment from the prom. He said I might not be allowed to graduate with my class. He made it his personal responsibility to check my so- briety before school events. That's right, he stopped me at the door to the prom and demanded, "Breathe on my nose."

I was finally summoned to a showdown meeting in his of- fice, where he sat me down and said, "You baffle me, Clark. I see unlimited potential in you. And yet you squander it. You don't apply your obvious talents. Why? I just don't get it."

His words stung. I was already disappointed in myself, drink- ing myself numb to ease the pains of insecurity and guilt and self-loathing. I didn't realize it then, but I could have used that opportunity to explain what haunted me. I just didn't appreciate the menace that my secret posed to a healthy future. Besides, I was just a kid, too busy running from the pain to stop and under- stand it. So, once again, offered a chance to share—and possibly purge—my demons, all I could do was blink back tears, swallow hard, and shrug my shoulders.

But with that missed moment, my future was sealed. The *adolescent me* was careening into adulthood on a mission of self- destruction. I wasn't the only one. With a serial pedophile in our little town, greater Stillwater was becoming a cesspool of secrets.

Take two of the guys closest to me growing up—my brother, Jay, and our next-door neighbor Jeff. We had all "wrestled" with the same pedophile scoutmaster. None of us talked about it. Not one of us shared any secrets, not even with one another. It would be decades later before we discovered that Jay and I shared the same dark secret.

Most details about neighbor Jeff's experiences with Pegg died when he did in his early twenties of a self-inflicted gunshot wound. To his family, there had been obvious tensions between young Jeff and Pegg, dating back to a summer out-of-state fishing trip that ended abruptly. Then-teenaged Jeff called home collect and pleaded with his mother to wire cash immediately for his bus fare, for him to get away from Pegg.

When he got home a few days later, Jeff told his mom, "Don't ever let me go away with that man ever again." He offered no further explanations, but Jeff's family—like my father after hearing disturbing accusations against Pegg—had their own lingering questions.

So, it was a surprise to some when Pegg showed up uninvited among the first responders to the scene of Jeff's suicide. Pegg offered to assist the family in formally identifying the body. "Why was he there?" Jeff's sister Brenda still wonders.

Jeff's death was a blow to my family as well as to his own. We had grown up almost as siblings. We were the first to hear of the tragedy when Brenda ran to our house, hysterical and bloodied from her terrible discovery.

Three decades later, after Pegg's death, officials settling his estate discovered a yellowing newspaper clipping of Jeff's obituary. Brenda called it "a weird thing" that Pegg had kept it with his most important personal papers, locked in his safe-deposit box.

As for me, college offered my first chance to start over—to forget the past, to escape the constant presence of Dennis Pegg, to reinvent myself in a new place with new friends and new opportunities.

But when I packed for my new life in Boston as a freshman at Northeastern University, I still carried the same old fears and guilt and insecurities.

Part III

MANHOOD

Computer science studies were big in the mid-1980s, and since I started college with no particular professional interests, I followed my father's advice to take computer science classes. It lasted a few months before I switched to business studies. It was the right choice. I was a natural—dean's list, teachers' favorite. It also left me with time to play. I quickly fell into a regular routine: Four days of focused study followed by three days of parties. I'm told those parties were a blast—kegs, booze, pot, and cocaine. Through most of those three-day blowouts, however, I was blackout drunk. My life might have seemed like a single guy's dream, with one-night stand after one-night stand. But, like my alcohol consumption and my early cocaine use, my sex life had a manic quality to it. I might have been predisposed to addiction. But after being raped, well, I had a lot of insecurities to deal with. For me, sex wasn't about love or companionship. It was all about proving my manhood—to myself.

Chapter Nine

TORNADO STRUCK

During my four-day focused study periods I tended to sneak off and isolate myself in the Ell Center, Northeastern University's study hall. It was generally the last place my party pals wanted to spend time. Its spacious surroundings were quiet and well lit, with plenty of tables suitable for individual or group deliberations. I liked to take over one of the midsize tables—ideally, a four-seater—and have it all to myself. No distractions, no diversions, for 100 percent concentration on my academic life. It was effective, too—until the sudden appearance one day of a blond stranger. She slammed down her backpack on one of the empty chairs and plopped down in the other one across from me, swinging both legs over the arm in an exaggeratedly casual pose, before launching into a breathless soliloquy:

"Hi, my name is Lisa. I'm a freshman. I'm from Orangeburg, New York. We're Jewish, my parents are very strict, so I'm glad to be on my own now. I've got two sisters. One's older. The other's still in high school. They follow all the rules. I love having fun. You might say I'm the black sheep of my family. And, oh, by the way, do you ever speak?"

At least, that's how I remember it. Lisa Kaufman was like a storm that had just blown into my life, like no woman I'd ever met. When I finally spoke, I didn't hesitate to express my interest: I invited her to our weekend party. She came and found me in the crowd. Later, we shared our first kiss. It was the beginning of a special, but complicated, friendship—filled with passion and estrangement, affection and alienation, harmony and heartbreak. It must have been among the unlikeliest relationships in the annals of modern romance.

Still, despite our intimate connection, my secret remained my secret. What I wouldn't share with my father or mother, not with either of my siblings, and not with my best pals at home or in college, I was not going to share with the girl that made me so happy that I could almost forget Dennis Pegg. Almost.

After a year or so, I brought Lisa home one summer to meet my family. Later, she spent a Christmas break with us in Stillwater. She became a big sister to my niece Kim—my brother's seven-year-old daughter. They spent time together, and Lisa read stories to her. My parents loved Lisa's affable nature and playful personality. Whether I acknowledged it or not, she was steadily and without ceremony becoming part of my family.

I kept ignoring the most obvious question: *Where is this relationship going?*

Eventually, with college graduation looming, lots of other

questions were stacking up, too: *What should I do for a living? Where? With whom?* Some of those uncertainties worked their way into my conversations with Lisa, who was observant enough to notice something was amiss with me. It could come out at dinners, on dates, even in bed.

"Hello? Hello, are you there?" she would ask me. "Where did you just go?"

She sensed my thoughts wandering, like something was on my mind that I wasn't sharing with her. I wondered how she could tell, but I always denied it. "You're imagining things," I insisted.

Pressure to commit to our relationship and a career, even to a routine job, had me at times in the grip of a silent panic. My most reliable answer to the pressure was booze or cocaine. It still worked to ease my angst and insecurities. But the trouble with substances was that they wore off.

A couple of weeks before graduation I got a call from the New Jersey–based pharmaceutical giant Johnson & Johnson. I was graduating cum laude, and one of my business professors had recommended me. The man at J&J invited me to come in for an interview.

I said I'd get back to him. I never did.

Instead, I went into business with my father and one of his friends. Dad, who had for years been a successful factory rep in the tire-and-rubber industry, put up the investment money to open a tire-retreading shop serving trucks along the Interstate 80 corridor. Dad's start-up investment—something in the realm of six figures—solved my immediate career dilemma. I moved back to Sussex County, back to the old neighborhood

I shared with my family—and, inevitably, with Dennis Pegg. I found myself surrounded again by reminders of my buried secrets.

Those secrets grabbed me by the throat in the spring of that first year back. My eighty-year-old widowed grandmother was raped and murdered at her home in Naples, Florida. The news was devastating to the whole family. To me it acted as a reminder that God didn't seem to give a damn about the Frederickses, young or old. It couldn't but trigger my memories of Pegg, and a rage that caught me by complete surprise. I didn't want to see my friends. I didn't want to see Lisa. I hid out in my room, drinking alone and trying not to imagine my grandmother's suffering, even as I tried to forget my own trauma.

Getting to work was a helpful diversion. Although I wasn't particularly challenged, or even interested, in the fine points of marketing tire retreads to truckers, we were a growing business that demanded my attention. I was making sales calls one day, driving a delivery truck the next, then filling in for a sick employee in the shop the day after that. I was doing it all—from shaking hands to getting them dirty. It kept me focused, and our early success was satisfying.

The money was good, too. I had plenty for booze and parties and whatever a twentysomething guy from Stillwater might want. I was doing more than all right. Still, I was floundering, trying to figure out why I wasn't happy and, I guess, what I wanted to be when I grew up.

One person got tired of waiting for me to figure it out. The blond tornado that had touched down at my Ell Center table six years earlier, then befriended my whole family, was ready for me to settle into a permanent and exclusive relationship.

"What are we doing?" she finally asked. "Are we just going to keep talking about talking about it, or will we ever take the next steps?"

She was asking that I commit to more than a "friendship." It was a relationship requiring devotion and total trust. I couldn't explain my hesitation then—not to her or to myself—but my boyhood trust in special friend, Denny, had ended in the worst kind of betrayal. It left me wary of ever being vulnerable again. And the still-raw trauma of losing a saintly grandmother to violence only added to my reluctance to risk loving anyone enough to be hurt again.

"I can't do it," I told Lisa. "Not at this time in my life. I just can't do it."

"Why? What's wrong, Clark?" She seemed genuinely at a loss. And I couldn't tell her. So, two years after I finished college, we broke up without so much as a harsh word. Her last love letter ended, *I hope we can always be friends.*

Like all her notes over our years together, this one was full of heart and understanding. It left me asking myself the same question: *Yeah, Clark, what the hell is wrong with you?*

Chapter Ten

OUT OF THE PAST

After college, I liked to think my parents were happy to have me home—literally. I moved back into my old bedroom. It turned out Mom was nursing some private regrets, needling my father about how the tire-retreading business didn't seem to her the best use of my "excellent education." Eventually, her complaints became more open, some version of "He could've been working for Johnson & Johnson, for crying out loud!"

That family tension only increased as business differences arose between Dad and his partner, a retired state police officer, Joe Colligan. In exchange for my father's big start-up investment in our retreading shop, Joe and I were expected to buy our rubber from Dad and the Goodyear company, which he represented. It was a premium, more expensive grade, and cheaper brands were available. So, when Joe insisted on stocking an inventory that included the cheap stuff, Dad was furious.

I was stuck in the middle, feeling like a captive or a pawn in their game—or, deep down in my psyche, like that kid I'd been back when I couldn't escape my molester. After all those years, feeling trapped still triggered my panic response.

Nothing I could do seemed to make a difference. I got into screaming matches with Joe as I defended my father's interests. I grew resentful of my father for pressuring me to do more on his behalf. Mostly, I was in constant conflict with both partners—until I finally walked out.

Goodbye tire retreading. Hello, Wall Street! I aced the licensing tests to land a job with the ninety-five-year-old financial firm First Investors Corporation. However, this would also mean a daily two-hour morning commute into lower Manhattan and a two-hour evening commute back to Stillwater. In between, I was to work the phones trying to sell various financial products, from annuities and mutual funds to bonds and life insurance.

It was hardly a dream job. I greeted day one with even less enthusiasm than the tire-retreading business. It started around a conference table—me and about a dozen fellow trainees about to get our first assignments. One of our new bosses came into the room with a cart full of fresh, fat New York City phone books. He circled the table, dropping the heavy volumes with a resounding *thwomp* on the mahogany tabletop, one for each of us.

"You—! Turn to the B section. . . . You—! Take the people under C. . . . You, Fredericks, you're calling every name that starts with D. . . ." And so it went—our initiation to the boiler room and cold-call hell.

I made it work for a couple of years, mainly because I was finally able to do the job from home, working with clients in the field. That minimized my commuting into Manhattan to a couple days a week. Then I quit the job and the commute altogether to work as an independent financial broker, but that held my interest only a short time. I quit again, this time to try my luck in construction and real estate investment—in other words, flipping houses.

Using a small inheritance from my grandparents, I bought an old, run-down farmhouse in a commercial area of Newton, set among business outlets and the state police barracks. Every lesson I learned, I learned the hard way. After replacing old floors and painting the interior, I had to do it all over again when a hard freeze burst the plumbing and flooded the house. My first customers, a nice couple that signed a rent-to-buy contract, stiffed me on the rent and moved out in the middle of the night—after trashing the place. I was lucky to get my savings back after working most of a year to break even.

I quit that job, too, leaving me on the verge of my thirties unemployed, unchallenged, and unfulfilled. It was one evening in that period when I brought some of my buddies to a favorite bar in Newton. We were looking for beer and single women as the bartender slid our first round of cold ones down the bar.

"Hey, Clark, how ya doing?" boomed a familiar voice. I turned to face Dennis Pegg. He was patting me on the shoulder like we were best friends. "How's your family?"

I stopped breathing. I was trapped in a crowded bar, my jaw clenched. Every muscle in my body seemed to seize up into a sudden mass of rigidity. I considered trying to gulp down that first drink but feared I might choke. My brain filled with noise. I don't remember what I said, if I said anything. But before I knew it, Pegg was heading back to his seat, leaving me coughing, sputtering, and trying simply to breathe normally.

"We gotta go," I growled to my pals. Then I chugged my beer.

"What?" they all grumbled. "We just got here!"

"We gotta go," I insisted. And since I was the driver, the guys reluctantly threw back their own beers while I fumbled for a lame excuse. "There's no chicks here," I offered. "I know a better place." That seemed to satisfy them. At least, they all followed me out the door.

Driving away, I tried to explain my reaction to myself: *What the hell just hit me? What happened to my breathing, my muscles, my mind?* The physical response had been completely involuntary. But deep down I knew exactly what had hit me. It was my past.

Chapter Eleven

ADDICTIONS

I kept changing careers all through my twenties with little more care than I changed shirts, but I remained serious and committed to partying. Meeting and seducing women became both my real job and an addiction. It also filled a void. The flirting and the thrill of the chase were real-time tests of my manhood. The one-night stands had the added benefit of distracting me from my loneliness and self-doubts—and from my still deeply embedded guilt for "letting" a man rape the *twelve-year-old me.*

Some of those random romantic encounters turned into relationships, but they rarely lasted more than a few months—never long enough for me to feel vulnerable. I was incapable of being open and honest. I never shared secrets and always shied away from emotional intimacy. I ran away whenever I felt someone getting too close, just as I had fled an emotional commitment to Lisa after college.

Jaime would last longer than any of my other post-Lisa relationships. She was divorced, and on a cocktail of prescription
pills and alcohol. By then I was drinking heavily, too. Our addictions only added to the turbulence of our affair. When things
started to fall apart between us, Jaime arranged for couple's
therapy. Reluctantly, I went along.

Almost immediately into the counseling, Jaime revealed that
she had been sexually abused as a child. I was stunned. What an
opportunity for me to speak up, to share our traumas; to bond
over common pain and suffering and guilt and self-loathing.
Yet, I just sat there as she poured out her soul while I portrayed
my childhood like some kind of old-time, feel-good TV sitcom.
"What were you, the Beaver Cleaver family?" she finally complained. No one noticed that I was on the edge of a panic attack
whenever talk turned to her history of molestation—one foot jig-
gling nervously while I kept checking the time to see how much
longer before the session ended.

On another occasion, Jaime and I were driving to dinner with
friends when we pulled up to a stop sign on Route 94 and waited
for a pickup truck to clear the intersection and turn left, passing my driver's-side window. It was Dennis Pegg at the wheel. I
erupted with a string of profanities, spitting on the floor.

Jaime was alarmed at my reaction to say the least. "Who
was that?"

I had never told her anything about Pegg. And the sudden
encounter on the road had given me no time to measure my
response. I answered with a dismissive wave and said, "It was
Pegg."

"What? You mean my friend?" Jaime had a friend named Peggy.

"No, dammit! Dennis Pegg!"

My answer did little to clear up Jaime's confusion. I was still in a rage.

"Yeah? So, who's that? What's the big deal?"

I shook my head and tried to calm down, calling him "some scumbag I know."

We continued on to the dinner with our friends, where I immediately started pounding down drinks until I was so drunk that Jaime had to drive us home.

I finally fled that relationship, too.

The *party-animal me* always felt under pressure to stay fit, or at least appear to be virile and masculine. Unfortunately, booze tended to have an equal and opposite effect on whatever I was trying to achieve with my gym membership. That's when I discovered steroids. I hesitated at first, unsure whether to mix such powerful drugs with my heavy alcohol consumption. But a couple gym buddies got me supplied. And beach season was coming.

What a transformation. In weeks I was looking lean and mean, like some Jersey version of Arnold Schwarzenegger. *I loved me—* loved my new self-confidence, the way I looked, the way I felt about my body. For the first time in my life, I didn't care if people saw me with my shirt off. My scar—the one Pegg had touched and that I still blamed, at least in part, for opening me up to his sexual abuse—was no longer a source of shame or inhibition.

There was, however, a big downside to steroids. When I went off the pills, my muscles seemed to evaporate. I went from

Schwarzenegger pumping iron to Samson after his haircut. The only option was more pills, more time in the gym, less time for other urgent pursuits, like parties and women.

As much as I loved my so-called real job flipping houses, I needed a reliable income if I was going to stay on the party circuit. My brother came to my rescue. He was in the tire-retreading business, too—not in a partnership with our dad, but still in the cutthroat, competitive world of rival tire shops fighting to profit from a hot and dirty business. Jay needed someone he trusted who also knew the business. I was both.

But I had to ask myself, *Working again in tire retreading? Really? Working again with family? Really?*

The business itself had gotten no more appealing in the years since I'd walked away from it. Day in and day out, this was life in the shop: you're taking big truck tires, grinding off whatever tread remains on the original, then attaching a new tread that's bonded to the old tire by "cooking" it at more than two hundred degrees Fahrenheit. Yeah, glamour wasn't in the description. But the pay, though modest at best, would be steady.

For my big brother and for a little temporary income, I decided to give it a shot. I'd help him out for a few months and pocket some change. That was in 1995. I would still be with him sixteen years later.

The fact is that I was bored with my life. Sleeping around hadn't led me to the love of my life. It hadn't even filled that hole in my soul—or eased that creeping feeling that my life might be of no more value than those worthless sunfish down by the dam. I needed a new distraction.

I picked gambling. Soon after joining my brother's business, I took a weekend break and drove to Atlantic City for a day at the casinos. I wanted to see what it was like to risk some of my new income. During a previous visit, I had only played the slot machines. This time, I planned to test my blackjack skills, previously applied only to games with pals for nickels and dimes. But this would be no buddy trip. I went alone. I told no one.

It was another kind of challenge to my manhood. How daring was I? Would my cool under pressure attract femmes fatales or gastric ulcers? Was I more James Bond or Rodney Dangerfield? One thing was almost certain: no accidental encounters were likely with Dennis Pegg at any casino bar.

Two hours into my late-morning drive, the anticipation of getting lost in games of chance already had my palms sweaty and my heart racing. I thought I was excited about gambling. Later, I would understand the real power of a gambling addiction. It was no different from all the others—the women, the drugs, the alcohol. But, at least for a time, it promised what I craved the most: escape.

Chapter Twelve

HOOKED

I pulled into the first casino with easy parking—Harrah's—and walked straight to the bar for a beer while I soaked up the sights and sounds around me. It was dazzling. Lights blinking or pulsating, bright or dim, were all part of the excitement and entertainment. Most of the sound was from slot machines or occasional whooping winners around the craps table. Big-breasted barmaids roamed the floors with drinks. It was beautiful. And not a clock visible anywhere on the gaming floor.

What a great place to lose track of time and place and worries of every kind. *Let the forgetting begin.* I bought another beer and moved to a blackjack table that required $5 minimum bets, peeling off twenties for a seat behind a modest $100 stack of chips. I hoped no one noticed, but my hand was shaking as I wagered my first pair of $5 chips.

Just minutes later, I was a winner. My hand didn't shake when I wagered the next $10—and won again. Other players offered friendly advice: "You're hot. Raise your bets." I put down $25 on the next one. And won. I bumped it up to a $50 bet and ordered another beer. I played for two hours before a string of losses reminded me that, eventually, the house always wins.

Enough. I had satisfied my need for an adrenaline fix. And I was a winner, too. The dealer counted my chips. I cashed out with $1,800—a two-hour profit equivalent to more than two weeks' wages at my brother's tire shop. I was feeling good about myself for the first time in months, maybe years. I knew I had to try this again.

A couple weekends later, I was back, this time risking a $200 stack of chips. Again, I got winning hands from the first deal. This time, success came with a lot of advice—people yelling at me to double down, split, or hold, or whatever. I was confused and flustered. It was nerve-racking. So many opinions and different options were coming at me loud and furious. Enough! I cashed out.

Again, my stack of chips had grown—this time from $200 to $2,200. It would have taken me a month and a half to match that in salary back at the shop. Again, I felt good. I felt lucky. I even felt smart, smart enough to realize I had to know the game better.

Back home I launched a crash course studying blackjack to learn its strategies and tactics—with special emphasis on understanding the odds. I bought a small library of books by experts and professional gamblers, along with extra decks of cards and dice.

Dice? One thing I had noticed at the blackjack tables was how boisterous the crowds were around the craps tables—players and animated bystanders all shrieking and hollering as one.

I knew only that craps involved rolling dice. But it sounded like one big celebration, so I included craps in my gambler's education. It turned out to be an intense six-month tutorial on both games—all of it self-taught in the quiet privacy of my bedroom.

Yeah. I was hooked.

Even before testing my new gaming literacy, I knew gambling was my new drug. I didn't have to share my adrenaline rush with anyone. I could get high without medical prescriptions or risking my health or facing illegal-possession charges.

The isolation, the solitary play, the focus on the next card, the next bet, whether to split, hold, or double down—it was all part of its powerful seduction. It was like a party with no social obligations. No waiting for invitations or permissions or assistance. For hours at a time, my only relationship was with the gaming gods and the odds. My only commitment was to buy chips, win or lose.

To get myself back into live gaming action after so many months of study, I planned a solo return to Atlantic City. I landed this time at Trump's Taj Mahal hotel and casino, then the ultimate playground for East Coast gamblers on the city's Boardwalk.

I passed up the $5 and $10 blackjack tables. Too tame. I needed more dope, more adrenaline, so I slipped into a chair at the $25-minimum table. Feeling better educated and more than a bit cocky, I bought $500 in chips.

And I resumed my winning ways. Soon I was making $100 bets. During the next four hours I bet more on one flip of a card than I made in a week at the shop. I cashed out ahead by $8,000 and my pockets filled with chips and $100 bills. An old briefcase in a closet became my deposit box.

A couple more Saturdays followed at the Taj Mahal, with consecutive cash-out winnings that grew from $17,000 to $27,000. It got me an introduction to casino management. They handed me a special key to the hotel's private lounge on the fiftieth floor. Its muted atmosphere was the opposite of boisterous—a relaxed silence gently ruffled by clinking crystal, live jazz on the baby grand piano, and soft-spoken waitresses in sexy tuxedos taking complimentary orders.

Steak and lobster dinner, Mr. Fredericks? It's on the house. Would you care to start with champagne? Try a bottle of Dom Pérignon on Mr. Trump.

It was like living a fantasy. I sure wasn't in Stillwater anymore.

I was still the same insecure working guy from small-town New Jersey. I was barely thirty, and if anyone looked closely, I probably had rubber-tire residue under my fingernails. And yet, I was hanging out with rich, manicured high rollers and gambling heavies from around the country.

What could possibly go wrong?

Chapter Thirteen

THE *BIG-SHOT ME*

Who knew that taking so much of the casino's money would make me one of its favorite people? Besides the private lounge, I was being offered endless inducements to come back— free hotel suites, free limousines, "shopping spree" giveaways at hotel stores. And not only from Trump's Taj Mahal. I seemed to be in demand all over town. Hosts from Harrah's, the Hilton, and other Atlantic City casinos reached out offering me VIP seats at an Eagles-Giants game in Philadelphia and golf dates at the best courses in Jersey and tickets to shows and personal introductions to famous sports figures. Then Bally's flew me to Las Vegas for a fully comped weekend. My credit was pristine, like that of the Johnson & Johnson junior exec I never became. My signature at various casinos was sufficient for cash advances beyond my annual take-home pay at the shop.

During one particularly good-mood drive home from the Boardwalk, packing more than fifty thousand fresh casino dollars in my pockets, I slammed on the brakes and pulled a U-turn after passing a Harley-Davidson showroom. Inside, I found the machine of my dreams: a blue-trimmed white beauty, the 1997 Heritage Springer with wraparound fenders and fringed saddlebags. Not for sale, they told me. It was already promised to another customer.

I immediately opened bike-side negotiations, reaching into my pockets and systematically pulling out crisp wads of hundred-dollar bills. Somewhere around $21,000 I owned it— my first Harley and the new love of my life.

So many good things were happening. After a while, I just couldn't resist showing off to those closest to me. For my mother's sixty-eighth birthday that year, the Taj comped my entire family—Mom, Dad, sister Holly and her husband, brother Jay and his wife, and me—to high-roller suites. We got fancy dinners and lots of champagne on the fiftieth floor. And we made our round trip from Stillwater in luxury aboard a supersized limousine, courtesy of the house.

It hadn't yet dawned on me that with all this VIP treatment the Taj and all the big casinos were in the business of grooming gamblers—high-rolling fanatics and addicts alike—to keep us all coming back. They knew the odds that their gaming tables would eventually have their way with us. In the meantime, we had this special relationship with the house, sharing insider access, exclusive benefits, secret keys, and hosts offering connection and friendship and a sense of belonging to even the most insecure—like me.

On the ride to Atlantic City with my family that day, we drank and joked and celebrated Mom. I handed out $500 in Taj

Mahal chips to each of the six to gamble as they wished. Dad and Jay wanted to learn craps. And I was just the big shot to teach them.

Too bad that the former *altar-boy me* had forgotten the Sunday school thing about pride going before the fall.

We got on the first open table we found. Eager to impress, I started betting . . . big. I was violating the first commandment of my personal gambler's bible: *Be patient until you get a feel for the table.* But, no, I did the equivalent of a running cannonball leap into a cold swimming pool. I lost $30,000 in fifteen minutes.

I was more peeved than embarrassed. "I'm gonna play some blackjack," I told them, trying not to reveal any hint of self-loathing. But I had to quickly add, "Alone!"

Retreating to the privacy of a high roller's room, I signed for a $20,000 marker (a cash advance) and almost immediately blew through that, too. Out of cash again, I retreated this time to my room and its premium-liquor supplies, hoping a stiff drink would make me feel less like a loser. I was already an expert at hiding secrets, projecting false fronts, and keeping my emotions bottled up. But I would need that when the family reconvened in the Maharaja Room later that evening on the fabulous fiftieth floor.

"Hey, Clark—how'd you make out at blackjack?" I was asked minutes into cocktails, overlooking the city lights. *Loser* seemed the underlying message to me. It was not a question any seasoned gambler would ask another gambler. Unfortunately, no one in my family knew gambling etiquette.

"Up and down," I answered evenly, with a nonchalant shrug and a forced smile. Translation: *I lost, and I don't want to talk about it.*

After dinner I sneaked back down to the blackjack tables, put another $25,000 cash withdrawal on one of my credit cards, and lost it so quickly that I headed to bed before midnight, down a whopping $75,000. Worst gambling day to date.

I did, however, still have substantial winnings stashed around my room at home—cash and chips in the hundreds of thousands of dollars in sock drawers and the old briefcase in my bedroom closet. That night was a bust, but by the end of that year, I'd bounced back dramatically, at the expense of a craps table at Bally's Atlantic City. In a single day the boost to my closet briefcase would be more than $150,000.

Winning was always a pleasure, like a good one-night stand. But it didn't mean I'd be happy the next day. At the tables, I never gave Dennis Pegg a thought, but cashing in a winner didn't drive away the lingering effects of those secrets, either. I was still that scared, betrayed, raped little boy. And if winning wasn't buying me a happily-ever-after kind of life, it was at least buying time for me to face those issues.

Practically speaking, however, all that cash accumulating in my closet did pose some immediate dilemmas. For one thing, it wasn't secure. It wasn't earning a dime. And it was likely taxable. So far, I hadn't lost nearly enough to offset that much income.

Some friend told me that if I made relatively small cash deposits into my bank account—something under $10,000 each— the banks wouldn't flag my surging income to federal or state tax authorities. Needless to say, my adviser was no certified public accountant. Still, I began slowly moving nearly a quarter million dollars, at the rate of about eight or nine thousand every week or so.

The balance on my little Bank of New York checking account, where I deposited my paychecks—and where I used to routinely reconcile income and outgo to avoid bouncing checks—boomed to six figures. I opened stock-trading accounts at Merrill Lynch and with another local investment broker.

I also went back to playing the odds more frequently. My old briefcase was filling up again. But I was still a $40,000-a-year grunt in the tire-retreading business, gambling like a guy on the *Forbes* list of billionaires. Something was wrong with that picture, and it would soon be too wrong to ignore.

One afternoon, coming home from the shop, I stopped at my curbside mailbox to bring in the usual assortment of letters, bills, and advertisements. Reaching in from the cab of my truck, I found an extra item left prominently atop the mail: a particularly ominous business card.

"This can't be good," I told my steering wheel.

There was a note on the back: *Mr. Fredericks, please call me immediately.*

The card was embossed with a gold badge insignia. It included the address and phone number of some special agent with the U.S. Internal Revenue Service—Criminal Division.

Chapter Fourteen

A THOUSAND VOICES

M y potential tax liabilities turned out to be of secondary interest to the IRS Criminal Division. They suspected I was laundering cash for such nefarious types as drug runners or terrorist gangs. To prove otherwise, I was in for the audit from hell. I braced myself.

It was also around this time, late in the 1990s, that I was invited to sample a booster dose of gambling thrills—just in case I was getting bored at the high-roller casino tables. A local saloon owner said that he had told some people about me—gamblers, people with "heavy connections—mob guys." Some of my wins and losses had become the stuff of legend around our little county, at least in gambling circles. Casino hosts were fighting over me; why shouldn't the bookies be, too? Lucky for them, I was always open to new risks.

"They want you to know," the bar operator told me, "I mean, if you're interested, that they do sports betting. No limits. Absolutely no ceilings or floors." He gave me a phone number that would automatically expire in a few days. I dialed it right away and got a voice straight out of Brooklyn. When we hung up, I had a code name: Gold Twenty-Three.

This was fantastic. No more waiting for the weekends and a long limo ride to Atlantic City. I could bet every night on something—baseball, football, hockey, basketball. The research came to resemble a full-time job. There were morning sports pages to pore over, games to monitor at all hours across the country, and nightly booze-fueled strategy conferences with my buddies to share and debate our picks. Sports wasn't simply entertainment anymore. It was now my daily dose of adrenaline, more proof of my manhood.

The risks were modest at first, a few hundred dollars a game. But within a few weeks, the per game bets had jumped to $500, then $1,000. My biggest win for a week was $28,000. It was soon topped by my biggest loss: $34,000.

I was still taking those weekend trips to the Taj and Bally's to keep up my high-roller relationships with casino hosts. If I was missing for a few weekends, they might gently nudge me. The subtext clear: we want to see you at our tables.

Foxwoods casino in Connecticut was wooing me, too, with tickets to New York Giants games and seats in their luxury stadium suite. But showing my appreciation at their tables required some long drives across three states. They sent a limo for me and some friends. We got stuck in traffic on Interstate 95 and drank our way the last couple of hours to the casino. I lost $20,000 that night.

The intensity and frequency of my gambling never let up. I started picking up emotional tics, obsessive-compulsive traits. Superstitions replaced logic, the odds, the wisdom of my inner voice. For a while, I had to step on every crack along the sidewalk. Then I had to avoid them. I had to climb stairs at the shop in a certain way. When I got into my truck, I had to touch things in a certain order. When I got to the casinos, I had all sorts of rituals to avoid jinxing myself.

The stresses were piling up. So were my losses. Eventually, I noticed the steady decline of my cash reserves. I was funding much of my latest gambling action with debit card withdrawals from my investment funds. Of course, all I needed was one deluge of winning dollars to refill the reservoirs. Before the rains came, however, the balance in one fund dipped so low that it had to be liquidated.

Alongside these stressors was that of my dad's failing health. A decade or so earlier, when he had been in his fifties, he had suffered a couple of strokes and a heart attack. Doctors tried an experimental blood filtration treatment, but he contracted chronic hepatitis C. It became increasingly debilitating.

Mom was sure he could recover if only they spent more time at their condo in Florida. That meant I had the house to myself when they traveled. I had always tried to stay upbeat when they were home, give them no reason to worry about me. Yes, I was still living at home in my thirties, but I assured them I was going to get my life together any day. Of course, they worried anyway.

One weekday evening during a deep dive alone into a 750 ml bottle of Ketel One, I ventured out of my room to the kitchen, where I ran into my mom. I knew she blamed most signs of my wasted life—whether it was excessive drinking or gambling or lack of ambition—on a curable condition. I just needed true love. She picked this time to ask, Whatever happened to that pretty girl with the great personality, Lisa?

Yeah, I confessed, I sometimes wondered about her myself. Mom put her arms around me, and I inexplicably started to choke up, telling her, "I really fucked up, didn't I?" That's all I could squeeze out before my throat closed. For several moments I just stood there wrapped in my mother's arms as we cried together.

I had my own cure for such difficult and unwelcome emotions: Thursday nights with the guys, about a dozen motorcycle friends. We called it Steak Night. This became a regular diversion—me, my pals, and my true-love Harley on our weekly tour of biker bars and strip joints from the Jersey Shore into New York City. Most of my fellow bikers were, like me, occasional coke users and borderline alcoholics who loved to party.

On one of those Thursdays in 1999, I brought home a baggie full of cocaine. Alone in my room, I figured that I deserved a reward for getting home safely. I poured a drink and did a line, then thought to myself, *I don't have to be at work for another eight hours.* So, I snorted another line and finished my drink.

I couldn't sleep. My heart was pounding. I had the weird sensation that I was surrounded by people whispering, a thousand voices murmuring all at once. I tried to listen carefully, to detect the words—or at least to go to sleep trying. The sounds were captivating, then disturbing. Eventually I got up, turned on the light, did another line of coke, and had another drink.

Big deal, I thought, *I've still got seven hours.*

Auditory hallucinations, they were called. My first. They lasted all night. I don't recall a moment's sleep. When it came time for work, I was a mess. Groggy. Paranoid. Shaky. *Never again!* I lied to myself. Then I downed a glass of vodka and OJ and went to work. Alongside the usual business of the day, I had to find time and focus to pick my weekend sports bets.

It would result in one grand finale of a terrible week. I placed a series of bad bets, at $5,000 a game, that together racked up a one-week total loss of $40,000. I had to liquidate my second investment portfolio—and that just barely covered half the debt.

A disastrous eight-month run through much of 1999 had wiped out four years of casino winnings. Even my old briefcase was empty. That was bad, but there was still worse: I owed the mob twenty grand.

Chapter Fifteen

THE SCUMBAG

I was dead broke, nothing left but my good credit and a dilemma: Should I risk *that*? What if I got the mob to let me wager one more week on credit? One voice in my head objected, *Walk away, Clark. Cut your losses. Escape this wild treadmill while you can.* The other voice scoffed, *C'mon, Clark, go for it. Win it all back. You can do it. Don't go out a loser. Be a man!*

An internal debate raged on even as I dialed the boiler room number. It only rang once.

"Hey, this is Gold Twenty-Three. I've got to move some funds around. Any chance we can let my twenty g's ride another week?" Deep down I was hoping for quick rejection. It would've been so much easier.

Instead, the voice on the phone didn't hesitate: "Twenty thousand? No problem. You're good. Catch up next week."

Cue the funeral dirge.

Not only would I have to win the upcoming week's bets just to stay in the game, but I had to make up for last week's major losses. The result was a reckless round of panic wagering—each play bigger, bolder, and dumber than the last. All I achieved was to nearly quadruple my debt. I'll spare you the math: I now owed my bookies an impossible $77,000.

The good news: I knew my gambling days were over, done, finito. The bad news: I had to confess my insolvency to the gentlemen who had funded my financial disaster. I didn't know who, exactly, operated the sports betting outfit, but I was under no delusion that they might be members in good standing with the Better Business Bureau.

I rehearsed my pleas for mercy and a repayment plan. *Look, it's gonna take some time, but you know I'm a stand-up guy. I'll make it good. I'm sure we can work something out.*

One more time, I dialed the boiler room. It was morning, a bit earlier than usual for placing the day's bets, but still the phone only rang once. I introduced myself with practiced nonchalance.

"Gold! How the hell are ya?" The familiar voice seemed especially happy to hear from me.

No sniveling, I told myself.

"I got a problem, bro. I'm tapped out, not a penny to my name. I can't pay you guys a dime this week. What can we do?"

I finished to silence.

Finally, the voice said, "Ah, that's not my department, man. I'll have someone call you back. Just one thing—be sure to answer your phone." He sounded sympathetic.

"Sure!" I said, feeling strangely hopeful.

Click.

But I also felt tired. Exhausted from the manic pace of my life. Exhausted from the stress of four years risking huge sums at casinos. Exhausted from eight months of sports betting that had finally plunged me into overwhelming debt. Sitting there at my desk, waiting for that dreaded return call, I realized for the first time just how thoroughly, to-the-bone exhausted I was.

Ring! Ring!

My flip phone caller ID showed only RESTRICTED. I hesitated.

Ring! Ring!

It had to be my nameless, faceless phone friends reaching out from the sports betting world—someone, I hoped, with the authority to work something out, something we could all live with. I touched the green button to connect, and a screaming male voice exploded in my ear:

"You! Degenerate! Worthless! Scumbag!"

His suggestion that I should "find a way to get the money" came with a reminder of the stakes in this contest: "Or, your life will be going down the shitter."

Click.

I knew I couldn't run. I couldn't call the cops. And I couldn't just sit and wait. After a couple minutes quietly contemplating my future as an endangered species, I opened my phone again, dialing the only people I trusted for advice.

A pleasant voice answered, "Gamblers Anonymous."

Chapter Sixteen

GO ROB A BANK

I felt like a corpse at an autopsy. A small group of recovering compulsive gamblers under the direction of counselor Ed Looney were dissecting my life—mulling over every detail of my gaming history, what I owed the bookies, the tone and text of the threats, and what my friends and family knew about it all. This was later that same evening, after the screamer's call.

Ed and his group agreed: I was in deep shit. Of course, they put it more clinically. They said, "We believe that level of debt puts you at genuine risk." So they turned their scalpels to dissecting my personal finances, or what was left of them. I still had a job. They tried to balance my monthly income with my living expenses before carving out a repayment plan to chip away at that $77,000.

I was skeptical, knowing something about the cost of money: interest rates, also known in some neighborhoods as the juice, the vig—the loan shark's cut, in other words. It would never be pegged anywhere close to the Federal Reserve's prime rate. They ignored me and suggested I offer my debtors $400 a month.

"They won't be happy," Ed predicted. "But you have to stick to the plan."

The key, he said, was for me to make clear that I intended to make good, that I was not running away from my obligations, that I was not going into hiding. Others in the group vouched for the strategy based on their shared experience. I felt better, even a bit optimistic—until I got back to my truck later that evening.

The cell phone I'd left on the passenger seat showed two missed calls—both restricted numbers. No messages, none needed. Paranoia rode shotgun all the way home.

I slept with a gun by my bed that night. In the office, I kept a baseball bat propped against my desk. I wasn't running or hiding, but I was thoroughly spooked.

The call came in the next morning. I took a deep breath and tried for a friendly and relaxed demeanor: "Hello, this is Clark Fredericks."

"You stupid fuck! I know who the fuck I called."

I tried to be agreeable. "Yes, sir, I'm sure you do."

"You being some kinda wiseass, you little fuck?"

I tried to apologize but he cut me off.

"Listen to me closely, you fuckin' scumbag. You're done jerkin' our chain. You gotta find some fuckin' money or your health is in serious jeopardy."

He paused, so I seized the moment. "I appreciate your patience, but like I said, I've got no way of coming up with that chunk of change. I am, though, ready to start a monthly payment plan. Immediately. Four hundred a month."

Yup, as Ed Looney predicted, he didn't like it, showering me with enough f-words to make the boys back at Gamblers Anonymous cringe.

"Are you fuckin' insane? Four fuckin' hundred a fuckin' month? That don't cover the fuckin' juice you already fuckin' owe us. You don't have any fuckin' idea who the fuck you're fuckin' with here, do you?"

I wasn't trying to be flippant, and definitely not snarky, when I responded earnestly, "I've got a pretty good idea."

"No fuckin' way!" he shrieked, his decibels rising. "You obviously have no fuckin' clue, else you wouldn't be riskin' your fuckin' life this way."

But then he softened for a moment.

"Look, the people you owe are old men who sit at the cafés sippin' their espressos all day. If I gotta go to them and say that all you're willing to do is make a fuckin' monthly payment, what can I say, it'll be over for ya."

"I understand."

"Let me ask you a question," he resumed in a calm voice. "How come you don't borrow the money from your father? Your brother? Your fuckin' friends?"

I was ready with lines scripted by Gamblers Anonymous, and I delivered them with as much sincerity as I could muster: "This is my responsibility, not theirs. I'm not running away from it. I'm trying to handle this like a man."

The voice was unimpressed. "How fuckin' noble of ya. But let me tell ya something, when time runs out, you're gonna regret it. You only got one more week, you piece a shit. I suggest you borrow the money. Or go rob a fuckin' bank. Cuz if you don't have something next week, whatever happens to ya, you know, you brought it on yourself."

Click.

Absolute rejection. *Now what?* I continued to get daily calls for a few more weeks. The voices changed, the messages growing only more menacing. One made me recoil in disbelief:

"You will be paid a visit. We're sending a coupla big dicks to rape your little white ass."

I told myself it was just a cruel coincidence. There was no way the mob could have any inkling of my childhood abuse, no way its debt collectors could know to target my psychic wounds. But that day I couldn't avoid it. I thought of Dennis Pegg.

When another one of the callers reached my ailing dad at home, Dad came to me clearly shaken. "They called you a scumbag piece of shit who stole money from them, and the man said if I wanted you to stay healthy, I had to—"

"It's my responsibility, and I'll take care of it."

Dad just shook his head. "I gotta tell you, Son, I'm scared for you."

I was scared for me, too. But rural New Jersey was providing some unanticipated protection. Strangers stood out like trash in a garden. I was constantly on alert for out-of-towners, for unfamiliar cars, for unexpected sounds in the night. I also discovered the special coping assistance of cocaine.

A caller would growl something like "You're a fuckin' dead man." But then I could do a couple lines and be ready to party. Thanks to cocaine, I felt invincible. And thanks to cocaine, I was also losing track of the frequency of those calls.

Then, in a moment, I forgot the debts and the mob threats altogether. Dad collapsed suddenly, and we rushed him to the hospital.

Chapter Seventeen

BOY TO MAN

Mom spent days at Dad's bedside, at least until I got off work and relieved her. Nights I slept on a cot in his room, helping to keep him comfortable but also tuned in for any clues that might offer hope for recovery. The news was unrelenting and grim. The End Was Near. His kidneys and liver were shutting down.

Mom still wondered if moving him to Florida might restore his health. I felt like an ogre pointing out how much blood was visible in the catheters draining his kidneys. A very bad sign. And his pain was excruciating. He kept asking to go home. We arranged for hospice and moved a hospital bed into the living room.

For nearly a week my role was arranging his pillows, propping them up around him to ease a terrible backache, among so many other discomforts. Mostly, he slept thanks to the relief of painkillers.

One night I realized he was crying. "Dad, what's wrong? What can I do?" I gathered more pillows intending to rearrange his supports.

He could barely shake his head. "I'm not ready to leave yet."

I broke down crying with him, declared that I loved him, and begged him to "hang in there."

The next night, he awoke out of a long sleep and motioned for me to come close. He had gotten too weak to speak above a whisper, but he said, "Son, I need to tell you something."

First, a little Fredericks family history. In 1941 when my grandfather went off to World War II as a bomber pilot, he left my grandmother in Irvington, New Jersey, with their eleven-year-old son, Robert. She needed help raising and schooling the boy, who would become my father. She asked a local Catholic priest to, as she put it, "take care of Bobby."

We already knew that story. That's how Dad ended up in the care of a Catholic father while Grampa helped win the war. Now, on his deathbed, Dad told me the rest of the story.

"I want you to know that I was molested by that priest."

I was stunned. My father and I had been hiding the same secrets. In his heart of hearts, he must have known that I was, in fact, a victim, despite my repeated denials. And he wanted me to know that he knew.

I had no idea how to react—not to his molestation news nor to his tacit acknowledgment of mine. I had been so distracted trying to ease his physical discomforts, not to mention my own emotional ups and downs. I was still coming to terms with the lifetime of things I wanted to say and do before he left me. I just didn't see the opportunity, in this latest moment, to bond over our common traumas—finally, for both of us to be honest with each other.

I believe he was giving me permission to tell him the truth, inviting me to correct the record and tell him. Here's what I could have said.

Yes, Dad, Dennis Pegg did *touch me! I lied whenever you asked. I lied because I was afraid you might kill him and go to prison. I lied because I feared the man who would kill his own dog. I lied because I loved you. I lied because I thought I could handle this myself. You were right, he* did *hurt me. I'm still hurting. That fuckin' animal raped me.*

But after burying my secrets, the *thirty-three-year-old me* was no more ready to dredge them up than the *twelve-year-old me* had been two decades before. I just couldn't let go. Not yet. Certainly not that evening.

"I hear ya, Dad," I assured him softly. "Please, just take it easy."

I hoped he would sleep. He closed his eyes. A few hours later, he died. Robert Fredericks was sixty-nine.

After his funeral I went home to my room and cried alone in the family house that I continued to share with my widowed mother. In another month I would turn thirty-four years old.

There is no universal ceremony or custom, no commonly accepted point on a calendar, that marks when a boy becomes a man. But losing my father felt like that moment to me. Ready or not.

Part IV

MY GREAT DEPRESSION

Going into the twenty-first century, I was on some kind of endless losing streak: My dad had died. I was broke. The IRS audit had left me owing back taxes. I was trying to figure out how to file bankruptcy, but that required a lawyer I couldn't afford. Faceless gangsters still threatened to withdraw $77,000 out of my flesh and blood. I was a grown man still living at home, still working in the tire-retreading business that I found mind-numbing. And every day I felt light-years away from those heady times fifty floors up at the Taj.

Then the FBI called.

Chapter Eighteen

THE WIRE

I 'm calling about a fairly urgent matter," said a stranger's voice on the phone. He seemed abrupt, even pushy, but there were no threats. No f-words. He had already identified himself as a special agent with the Federal Bureau of Investigation. "I need to have a meeting with you. I'll be at your tire shop in Newton on Thursday three p.m."

"Whoa, whoa, whoa!" I needed more information than that. "What's this all about?" My angst was rising fast: *What do the Feds want with me? Did they have me on tape buying from my cocaine connection? Way too small-time. Did someone see me driving stoned? Hey, that's no federal offense!*

"Sorry," he said curtly. "I can't discuss anything over the phone. We'll talk Thursday at three in the afternoon. I suggest you be there."

"Yeah, sure." *What else could I say?*

Almost immediately I found comfort in a flash of simple logic: *Wait a minute . . . if they're coming to bust me, the FBI would never call ahead.*

But this was Tuesday. I had two days to sit and stew and second-guess myself. By Thursday afternoon I was completely on the edge. *What if this FBI guy is a ruse? What if I'm about to open my door to a couple of mobster "knee surgeons"?*

Nah, the goons wouldn't call ahead, either.

Still, I had to be careful and avoid getting lulled into a false sense of security. The daily threats to my health had become weekly, then monthly, and were now sporadic. I had not, however, forgotten the last words of the last caller: "You're a fuckin' dead man."

Shortly before the self-identified FBI man's scheduled arrival, I took my office baseball bat with me when I went out to move my truck. I intended to do my own surveillance, waiting to judge the pedigree of my visitor from a safe distance. But as the minutes ticked away, one thought occurred to me over and over: *I wish I had my shotgun.*

At precisely 3:00 p.m., I was relieved to see a late-model Ford Crown Victoria pull up just outside the office. It almost screamed *unmarked police car*. The clean-cut driver, its only occupant, stepped out wearing sunglasses and a dark off-the-rack suit. His hair was cropped short, conservative. I didn't need to see a badge to know a cop when I saw one. I left the baseball bat in my truck and intercepted him at the front door.

He was friendly enough, as it turned out. "Were you waiting in your truck on purpose?"

"I was."

"Smart."

But I wasn't looking for compliments, and I couldn't hide my impatience. "You didn't give me much over the phone. Made me nervous."

He gave me his business card, and I led him into the shop and upstairs to my office. That's where he pulled out his badge. We exchanged more niceties. He was grateful for the chance to meet with me, yada yada yada.

I finally cut to the chase: "What's this about?"

"Mr. Fredericks, the FBI has received intelligence, very reliable, from a confidential informant, someone in an organized crime family. A mob hit has been ordered on your life."

I smiled. It would have been impolite to laugh out loud, but I was thinking, *Tell me something I don't know.* He seemed surprised, maybe even disappointed, by my reaction—that I didn't show more alarm.

He tried to sum it up more dramatically: "Sir, your life is in jeopardy."

I explained that I hadn't heard from the debt collectors for some time.

"Really? Because we believe you are in immediate danger. We were told you've already had a gun put to your head."

"I've never had a gun put to my head. I've never met these people."

"Consider yourself lucky. When was the last time you heard from them?"

"I'm not sure. But it's been months. Two, maybe three or more. It's a blur."

That's when he got to what was behind this "fairly urgent" visit. Whenever those calls resumed, and he was sure they would, he wanted to know about it: "Would you consider wearing a wire?"

"You gotta be kidding!" There was no way that was going to happen. Still, I wanted to explain my situation. "Look, I'm responsible for the mess I'm in. I haven't tried to run or hide from anyone. I'm handling this. And I'm not looking for the FBI to come to my rescue, either."

In other words, *no deal*. We shook hands. I walked him back out to the street.

"These guys never go away," he said. "You may want to think twice."

And with that he was gone.

Back at my desk, I retrieved a plastic baggie with white powder that I suddenly needed to calm my nerves. *Bug the mob for the FBI? Yeah, suicidal stupidity!*

As bad as my life had been to that moment, I had at least not made things worse.

Chapter Nineteen

TAKEN FOR A RIDE

O ne reason I'd lost track of the time since my last mob call was that my phone had continued to ring incessantly with reminders of other obligations from other impatient creditors. I was behind on credit card bills—even those minimum payments were beyond me. I owed multiple casinos the equivalent of a six-month salary—each. There was that $10,000 I now owed in back taxes. At the same time, I was getting a daily earful from collection agencies. They were as unfriendly as the mobsters— absent, of course, the physical menace and crude vocabulary, but still offensive and disheartening.

I made a stab at working out repayment plans, but that proved especially frustrating. A few would consider some sort of compromise. But piecemeal settlements couldn't work. I finally filed notice of personal bankruptcy and left it to a federal bankruptcy judge in Newark to arbitrate and impose repayment amounts.

Still, it took four long, tightfisted years for me to settle every adjusted claim recognized by the court. I hadn't exactly found happiness, but I was relieved and feeling a renewed sense of independence. I moved in with a new girlfriend. I was still riding my Harley with the guys. I was also closing in on my landmark fortieth birthday.

I decided to do something nice for myself—shop for a bigger, flashier motorcycle.

Big Boar Cycles was a favorite in town. They did custom work for some of my friends and got lots of attention beyond Newton with high-profile designs for some NASCAR driver and a special tribute bike honoring blonde bombshell actress-model Anna Nicole Smith. I was so eager for one of those Big Boar custom jobs that I traded in my true-love Harley as the $10,000 down payment and borrowed another $33,000 with the help of my brother's cosigned loan for the balance.

As part of the deal, my bike frame would be painted by a guy recently recognized by *Easyriders* magazine as painter of the year. I topped off my splurge with an S&S 124 engine. The paint job was awesome.

I waited a couple weeks to drop into the cycle shop again to check on the progress. There was none. But Joe Rubino, the owner, assured me that a new transmission waiting on the office countertop would be installed shortly. Another week or so later I was back. The transmission had been faulty—or something. Joe pointed to a new S&S 124 engine that had just arrived and was on a workbench in the garage.

"That's your motor," he said. "We'll be putting it on your frame sometime this week."

"All right, cool!" I said, encouraged. But so far I saw no progress beyond the original paintwork.

Joe was hardly an affable businessman. He was about my size, six foot three, but bearded and heftier and heavily tattooed. He could've been a poster boy for some of the toughest biker gangs in the state. And he seemed to go out of his way to cultivate a no-nonsense, badass persona. But so did some of my biker buddies. It was all an act; I wasn't intimidated.

A month later, feeling hopeful that I'd get to see some progress on my bike, I walked into the showroom and found the same unfinished—and essentially unstarted—frame. No transmission. No S&S 124 engine. And this time, no Joe. I confronted one of his workers about the lack of progress.

"Look, man," the mechanic began, "I don't want to get in the middle of anything, but I installed those parts on other bikes. The transmission and the motor, they weren't even ordered for your bike."

"Joe told me they were mine!"

The mechanic shrugged. "Then he lied."

Hours later I confronted the big man in his shop. I wanted my money back. Joe didn't have it. I wanted my Harley back. Joe had sold it months ago. We screamed at each other. Nothing changed.

Then one night, Joe and every piece of inventory in his shop disappeared, carted away under cover of darkness.

This was betrayal on a level only the *twelve-year-old me* had ever experienced. Like the boy, I felt guilty for letting this happen to me. The *nearly forty-year-old me*, however, felt something much more than guilt and helplessness. It was rage—something dark and vengeful.

Rather than keeping this betrayal secret, I immediately went to the authorities and filed a criminal complaint. Later, I testified before a county grand jury. So did other victims. Joe was charged with third-degree theft. The case was dropped months later when the original prosecutor left the county, so I hired a lawyer, and we got a civil judgment against Joe's company, Big Boar Cycles. I never recovered one dollar.

During this period, I decided to burn off some of my frustrations and try to get healthy again—getting back on a workout schedule at the gym. That's where I ran into an old friend I had not seen for a while. He was so bulked up from recent bodybuilding work that I asked him, "What the hell are you taking?"

He was on anabolic steroids, he said, and shared the website he was using for mail-order deliveries. I was no stranger to the stuff. My first new buy required wiring money via Western Union to some Russian with the code name Draggon at an address in Kyrgyzstan. I shrugged off my doubts. *Hey, what the hell? You can lose plenty of money trusting someone right down the road in Newton, New Jersey.* Still, I kept the order down to a few hundred dollars. I also faked a name for myself—even though I used the same home address where I got all my mail.

Four weeks later, just as the website had promised, I found the steroids package in my mailbox, only it was from Greece. Encouraged by my success, I made a couple more modest orders. No problems, no delays.

I liked my progress at the gym, and I was ready to increase my pharmacological boosters. Besides, I was eager to use the more effective injectable versions of steroids. This time, I sent off more than a thousand dollars through Western Union to my Draggon supplier in eastern Russia.

A couple months later, after giving up on my biggest order, I found a letter waiting in my mailbox. It came to the right house but was addressed to my fake name. I knew exactly what this was about. It was the very official letter's return address that again caught my attention:

U.S. Department of Homeland Security.

Chapter Twenty

THE BOY LIKE ME

The DHS was brand-new to the federal government in the early post-9/11 era—an amalgamation of the old U.S. Customs Service, ICE (Immigration and Customs Enforcement), IBP (Immigration and Border Protection), the TSA (Transportation Security Administration), the Coast Guard, Secret Service, and more. But somehow, while rushing through a reorganization and printing a new letterhead, DHS still managed to pluck my little mail-order package from the vast international black market for steroids. And DHS did it despite my cleverly covered tracks using the fake name Ken Higgins.

Of course, not so cleverly, I had also provided them with my home address. When I pulled the DHS letter from my mailbox, I couldn't help glancing around and over my shoulder. Fortunately for "Ken Higgins" and me, the border protection bunch handling our case was reasonably polite about it. No mobster or collection agent ever opened one of our conversations with *Please be advised* . . .

After quoting various sections from the Code of Federal Regulations to remind me and "Ken" that importing controlled substances without a prescription was illegal, the letter kindly offered to send the steroids and paraphernalia directly if someone presented a copy of such documentation. Or, it added, I "may elect to request" that the government simply destroy the steroids this "one time" at no cost nor risk of prosecution.

My latest brush with a federal enforcement agency was essentially a first-timer's Get Out of Jail Free card. I considered it another bullet dodged.

Besides, my drug reliance was taking another direction after I wrenched my back working in the tire shop. Vicodin, a powerful opioid, was prescribed to control the pain. It helped me escape more than physical pain though; its intense highs and euphoria were addictive. Ultimately, it ushered in a long-running depression.

No question, my mental state had never recovered from my being so badly burned in the motorcycle deal. Everywhere were reminders of the sucker I'd been—loan payments for nothing, legal bills for winning judgments that would never be collected. Worst of all, no more true-love Harley, either.

I still looked forward to my weekly Steak Night outings, biker-barhopping with my bros. But my nights out were bikeless. They rode; I drove my pickup truck. Even having fun came with the seeds of depression. I blamed it all on a business betrayal. It was another wound to my psyche, to my manhood. And, as with the *twelve-year-old me*, that wound came loaded with guilt—and now a rage—that I just couldn't shake.

Drug-induced highs helped take the edge off. Alcohol-induced contentment helped. Sexual pleasure helped. Gambling diversions used to help, when I did that kind of thing. But escaping reality finally had a downside. If only the *former-altar-boy me* could have seen what was happening, he might have paraphrased a familiar truth from the Bible: *the wages of addiction are depression.*

I was starting to have trouble just getting out of bed. When I woke up stoned and in pain and dreading another day at work, simply getting myself to the bathroom was like climbing Mount Everest. Sometimes, I could barely swing my legs over the edge of the mattress without talking to myself: "C'mon, Clark. You can do it. . . . C'mon, feet on the floor . . . stand up, bro!"

I needed more than coffee. Booze for breakfast became a regular feature. It could be wine spritzers or champagne and orange juice. The cheap stuff—André's Extra Dry—was best for mixing. Sober starts to my mornings remained in steady decline. One afternoon, trying to shake the cobwebs from my brain, I ran into a QuickChek convenience store for a shot of caffeine.

I was pouring a self-serve coffee when I saw him. Dennis Pegg had just burst through the front entrance heading for the ice cream counter. I abandoned my coffee and slipped around behind a rack of snacks. *Maybe he won't see me. Maybe I can duck out when his back's turned.*

More customers filed in. A boy called out, "Denny, could you make mine a peach smoothie?"

I almost gasped out loud. The boy looked twelve years old. He looked just like I had. He called Pegg "Denny," just like I had done. And, God help me, I knew only too well what was going to happen to that boy—or maybe it already had—just like it had happened to me.

My jaw clenched. I was breaking out in a cold sweat. My whole body went rigid. I was fighting for breath, as if all the air had been sucked out of the store. The panic was only too familiar, coming at me straight out of my past, out of my childhood, out of that chair in Denny's living room.

I saw a clear path to the front door. Escape was now or never. I bolted for the exit and pushed it open—just as I heard Pegg's voice:

"Hey, Clark, where you going, buddy?"

Chapter Twenty-One

FREE-FALLING

My encounter with Dennis Pegg had dredged up decades of buried guilt and let loose all the repressed terror, the shock and confusion, and the betrayal. I roared off from the QuickChek in a rage, punching my pickup steering wheel, spitting phlegm and invective, cursing Pegg to the heavens: "You fuckin' piece of shit!"

For the next few days, I woke up thinking about Pegg. I fell asleep, when I could fall asleep, thinking about Pegg. I had no understanding yet of what PTSD was, but I *had* it—it was already, I would later realize, a roaring case of post-traumatic stress disorder.

Instead of therapy, I reached for the same cures I had come to rely on for pain and torment in my life: sex, drugs, and alcohol. I pulled a Friday all-nighter with a girlfriend, doing cocaine and booze well into the next day. The wise thing would have been to call in sick for work that Saturday. But my brother needed me. So, I gathered myself, freshened up, and headed for the shop more than an hour late.

Jay's mechanic, already out of sorts having to work the garage solo, greeted me curtly: "You're late and you look like shit." I told him where to stick his complaints, igniting a screaming exchange that brought my brother rushing out of his office.

"What's going on?"

The mechanic nodded at me. "He's late, and he's wasted."

I suggested that the mechanic mind his own business. But my brother sided with my critic. No doubt I *did* look like shit. and I *was* more than a little late, but I turned on my brother, telling him, "Go fuck yourself." Then, I walked out of the family business for the last time.

I was in free fall, on a plunge to rock bottom that was only gaining speed. I was just too screwed up to see it—or to care.

The college football season offered a brief diversion. I wasn't betting anymore, but I had Penn State fans for friends. One was biker buddy Joe Pepe, who offered some of us the ultimate tailgate party at the big Nittany Lions game against rival Ohio State. We made the three-hour drive in something like a tricked-out Winnebago motor home, complete with beds, a private bathroom, and a well-stocked bar. I have no idea who won the football game.

A couple of weeks later, former Penn State assistant football coach Jerry Sandusky was arrested on child sex abuse charges. The scandal shocked college sports. Sainted head coach Joe Paterno, the winningest coach in college football, announced he would retire under suspicion that he may have protected Sandusky instead of reporting him to authorities. A candlelight vigil for victims attracted a campus crowd in the thousands and more press coverage.

There was no avoiding Sandusky news. It was everywhere, from hometown newspapers to the network news shows. Ever since seeing Pegg with the boy at QuickChek, I'd remained fixated on memories of my own predator. My PTSD had nowhere to hide. To me, Sandusky was a Dennis Pegg on the national stage. I couldn't help wondering, *Am I one of ten victims, too . . . or maybe one of hundreds?* I wished Pegg a Sandusky-grade load of disgrace and humiliation, but only so long as I could be spared acknowledging I was one of his victims.

What promised to be among the most sensational child sex abuse trials in the twenty-first century was scheduled to start in June 2012. I wasn't ready to deal with it. There was just no way to shove Pegg back in the box where I'd kept him all those years. I was still estranged from my brother, too, still out of a steady job, and still chasing more drugs with more alcohol—still an emotional and physical mess. Friends worried about me, tried to get me out of the house, where I tended to hole up alone getting drunk and stoned and avoiding people.

On a Tuesday morning in mid-June, coming out of a three-day binge alone with cocaine and a bottle of Ketel One vodka, I awoke confused. A mysterious line of white powder remained on my dresser. *I must've fallen asleep before snorting that baby.* I immediately corrected my mistake and dropped back into bed holding the TV remote.

The morning news popped up on screen from live outside the Centre County Courthouse, where a reporter offered highlights from opening arguments the day before. Then the news show cut to video of Sandusky arriving at court earlier. At the sight of him, I sat upright in bed.

There he was: The child predator himself. I wanted to explode. Instead, I wrapped my arms around myself and started rocking, gasping for air, heart pounding, muttering expletives.

Sandusky was accompanied by a team of suits; his legal entourage, I figured. After stepping from his car, he waited for other suits to clear a path through photographers and onlookers. Then the defendant turned to the cameras and smiled. It looked eerily familiar.

Why do they all have that same damned smirk?

I finally exploded: "Jerry fucking Sandusky is smiling! That smug son of a bitch!" I was standing in my underwear now, spitting on the floor between curses, calling Sandusky every epithet in my amplified Jersey vocabulary.

The phone rang. It was a friend who wanted to get me out of the house. "How about lunch?" he said.

I didn't need food. I wasn't hungry. But I did need a friend. We agreed to meet at a Brazilian steak place a couple towns over.

Later, heading out to my truck, I ran into Holly. My sister was arriving at the house to have lunch with our mom. I guess I was scowling because she thought I looked mad at the world. It set me off, and I turned on her with a stream of harsh words and curses.

"Clark!" She stopped me. "What's the matter with you? I mean, you scare me. You're just not you anymore."

I told her to leave me alone, that I had a lot on my mind, and that, yeah, I was "really, really angry" and had every right to be. Once out on the highway, I finally started to relax.

My Tuesday was bound to improve.

Chapter Twenty-Two

MY HIT LIST

It turned out that my great depression, my long and lonely passage through a very dark place the past few months, had been the talk of the town, at least in certain circles. I was the former happy guy, the fun-loving party guy that had dropped out of circulation and morphed into the *antisocial me.* Out of public view I had become more of a doped-up-drunk-hiding-from-his-past kind of guy. Of course, no one knew the Dennis Pegg connection to me or to my moods. They just wondered, *What's happened to Clark? He's not fun anymore.*

That's how one of my biker bros, Joe Luchetti, put it. I think he blamed some of my personality changes on those old gambling troubles and mob threats. He always felt bad that he couldn't help me sort those out. He also knew the whole ugly story behind my lost Harley and how I got ripped off.

But getting back to some of my old haunts around town that Tuesday gave me a fresh shot of enthusiasm for renewing acquaintances. I ran into a cop friend and his girlfriend. A waitress said she was glad to see me. I caught up on local news from a favorite bartender. I was still stepping away to my truck from time to time for key hits of coke, but I wasn't thinking of Pegg.

After lunch at the steak place, I wandered around my old playing field of bars and pubs, in no hurry to hole up again back at the house. Besides, my eighty-something mom had just arrived home from her Florida condo and was feeling a bit under the weather. I figured I should stay out drinking a little longer. For her sake.

Approaching dinnertime, I stopped in at the Tuscany Bistro, another old favorite, in time to order a nice Italian red for the cocktail hour. I had been nursing my generous pour at the bar and catching up with the bartender when another friend—Don and his wife, Judy—came over to join me.

"Did you see who's in the dining room," Don asked, obviously eager to tell me.

"Someone I know?"

"It's your buddy Joe Rubino."

A slap in the face could not have wiped away my smile faster. The Big Boar Cycles owner was still in town, the guy who took my Harley and thirty grand was just a few steps away, still having a good time, still treating his family, still spending money he owed me and a few other trusting customers. I hadn't seen him since testifying at his bankruptcy hearing in Newark. I headed for the dining room.

Yeah, Joe Rubino was there, all right. I saw him. He didn't see me—not until I leaned over his shoulder and said quietly, "Hey,

Joe, when you gonna do the right thing, like be a man and pay me what you owe me?"

He was caught by surprise and embarrassed by it. He was also trapped in a vulnerable position. His only response short of trying to shove me away and making a big scene was to growl a couple of choice expletives. But I wasn't done. I impugned his manhood, let his family know that I thought Joe was dog shit, and that I felt sorry for the kid with Joe for a father.

In the clatter and hubbub of that noisy dining room, the Rubino family alone could hear me. I was content with that, and after holding my menacing position over Joe Rubino for just a moment more, I moved on.

Driving home, I called my biker bro Joe Luchetti to vent. I was still agitated and angry. He sympathized. What he did not do, however, was share any of his recent alarm or private musings about my prolonged depression and my antisocial isolation, things that concerned him and others.

"I think Clark's having a meltdown," Luchetti had worried aloud in so many words to more than one of our friends. "I'm afraid he's gonna kill himself, or hurt someone else."

We couldn't talk for long. Luchetti worked nights and had to hang up. I was passing another favorite bar, the Greeks, so I pulled in and parked. Their espresso-flavored vodka seemed to be calling me. Fortunately, I didn't have too much further to drive, so I figured I could have a couple rounds.

It was almost 8:00 p.m. when I got back into my truck. I knew another biker buddy, Bob Reynolds, was already on his way to my house. He was bringing his power-washing gear to clean my mother's cedar-shingle house the next day. I had loaned him a couple grand sometime back, and this service was in lieu of cash repayment. It was a gift for Mom.

Bob was going to stop over, drop off the equipment, and start the cleaning first thing in the morning. And since I wanted to offer him a nice bottle of wine that night, I planned one more stop—at the last liquor store before home off Route 94.

My friend Paul was shopping there, too. One of my best friends. Like Luchetti on the phone, Paul seemed concerned about me. He thought I looked out of it, agitated, even wild-eyed frantic. I shrugged it off and told him about running into Joe Rubino at the restaurant, about calling him a scumbag in front of his family. In the retelling, it occurred to me for the first time that night that Rubino might carry a grudge, that he might even track me down and show up at my door to retaliate.

"So, Paul, if I call tonight and say I've got a problem, be sure to answer your phone," I told him.

I got home a few minutes later and was still sitting in my truck when Bob Reynolds pulled in behind me driving his van. After we finished unloading his power-wash equipment into my garage, I invited him upstairs for a glass of wine. I interspersed sips of cabernet with cocaine hits and Xanax. I relived for him my restaurant encounter with "that motherfucker Joe Rubino."

Bob was leaning in and shaking his head. "Yeah, what a fucker. That Rubino must be number one on your hit list."

I shook my head. "No, Bob. Actually, he's number two."

I don't know what it was about that night—the wine, the Xanax, the coke. The friendly ear, the long day. My depression, anger, lack of sleep, self-pity. The sanctuary of my own home, all that Sandusky news, the gnawing memory of Pegg with the boy at the QuickChek. I will never know for sure. But in that moment, my defenses finally failed.

The secret that I had refused to share for more than thirty years, or under any circumstance, not even with my dying father or with my closest friends or lovers or counselors or siblings, not even Mom—I just said it, out loud, and in a steady voice.

"Number one on my hit list is the piece of shit who raped me as a kid."

And time stopped. We sat there staring at each other through a long moment of silence.

"Are you fucking kidding me?" Even Bob's expletive was spoken with reverence. "Who was it?"

"My Boy Scout leader, a lieutenant in the sheriff's department. I never told anyone. He was a big man in town. I was a boy. Who would believe me?"

Again, there was silence between us.

"He's still around?"

I nodded.

"Where does he live?"

"About three minutes from here."

We were thinking the same thing. It was only nine thirty on that long Tuesday night.

"He's a gun nut," I cautioned.

Bob stepped into the kitchen, and I handed him a black-handled, eight-inch steak knife. I reached under my bed and pulled out my wood-handled, six-inch hunting knife, the Scout knife I kept sharpened with that whetstone kit Pegg gave me for Christmas back in the 1970s. I slipped it out of its sheath. It was still precisely honed, just the way Denny taught me. I didn't need the sheath. I tossed it on my bedroom floor.

We chugged our wine and headed for Bob's van. He drove as I gave directions to the house where Dennis Pegg had raped *twelve-year-old me.*

Chapter Twenty-Three

HOW DOES IT FEEL?

Dennis Pegg still lived at 903-B Millbrook Road off the main street linking rural Stillwater to downtown Newton. The house wasn't visible from the road—the perfect hideaway for a serial pedophile. It was set back behind a stand of trees that allowed us to approach undetected up a long driveway with a ninety-degree bend in the middle. Bob shut off his headlights before we rounded that turn, giving us a direct view of Pegg's front door.

It was a warm night. The door was wide open, of course. After all these years, it was still true in Stillwater—no one locked the door. Only a screen door against insects stood between me and Pegg. From the shadows I could see he was watching television alone. But at the sight of him, I could feel my jaw tighten. Again. I was gasping for air. Again. My heart was beating out of my chest. My entire body was going rigid. Again.

What the hell? I wanted to yell at myself. *This was no time for a panic attack.* Then, I thought of Pegg with that boy at Quick-Chek. *Dammit! He's still doing it. He's still hurting kids! C'mon, Clark, you can stop him if you don't chicken out. What's the problem? You can't* still *be afraid of that man. How the hell can you sleep tonight if you run away again?*

Thirty years of repressed rage compelled me. I broke into a sprint toward the house.

Bob was right behind me, both of us flashing knives. I reached the screen door first. It wasn't locked. I yanked it open with such force that I pulled it off one hinge and left it dangling. One more step and I was standing in Pegg's house watching him watch television.

Pegg showed no alarm. He stayed seated in his comfortable chair. He simply turned and gave me a casual wave over his shoulder. "Hey, how are you?"

Maybe he didn't see the knife. Maybe he thought this was a social call. Maybe he thought we were friends.

"How am I, motherfucker? Let me show you how I am, Dennis," I sputtered, then started toward him.

That's when he jumped to his feet. But this was not his "little buddy" Clark coming at him. This was an armed and dangerous six-foot-three Clark. Neither Pegg nor any other person had ever seen this face, or this rage and hatred.

As I slashed wildly at him, I bellowed, barely coherent, "How does it feel raping little kids now?" I started chopping and stabbing in an explosion of fury. He backed away, but he wasn't giving up. It was a defensive move. He backed around the room, blocking my blade with his arms and hands, jabbing, counter-punching with a clenched fist, constantly moving, bobbing and weaving, looking for any offensive opportunity.

"How does it feel raping little boys now?" I repeated like some sort of mantra again and again with each swipe of my blade: "How does it feel raping little boys now, huh?"

And then his right hook landed a solid blow to my jaw. My knees started to buckle. I reached out and grabbed the front of his shirt to stop my fall, then threw my shoulder into him, driving him against a wall. I still had Pegg's shirt in the grip of my left fist as I plunged the hunting knife toward his chest. But I missed, instead driving that blade right through my own fist.

I don't remember feeling pain at that moment, but my left hand was suddenly useless. Blood gushed everywhere. Much of it now was mine. Still, I kept shouting, "How does it feel now?"

Through it all, Pegg never uttered a word. He made no plea for mercy, never begged to talk this over. His only sound was familiar to any country boy who ever hunted rabbits. It was a high-pitched squeal, the desperate shriek of an animal that knows it is doomed.

Pegg finally fell against a wall and slid down to the floor. His life was draining away. I knelt in front of him, panting from exertion, and looked into his vacant eyes. Leaning closer, I hissed in his face, "It's not so fun raping little boys now, is it?"

Then, I slit his throat.

Regrets? None. For all the abuse he had visited on me, for what he did to Mike Funari and to my brother, Jay, for neighbor Jeff and all the other crippled lives and untold suicides left in his wake, for all the kids he groomed and groped and terrorized, for the dog he beat into unconsciousness to intimidate me, I had no doubts: *Dennis Pegg deserved what he got, every wound, regardless of what it might cost me.*

When I stood up and surveyed the bloody scene, I saw Bob Reynolds was still standing in the front doorway. He was unbloodied, wide-eyed and in shock, still gripping his unused steak knife. I had one more mission, and I wanted to be alone. I told Bob to get the van.

The door to Pegg's bedroom was open. I stepped inside the unlit room, cleared my throat, and hurled a great wad of spit into the darkness. It landed on the neatly made bed where Dennis had raped me. Now, I was ready to leave. I didn't look back.

Outside, I found Bob in an apparent state of confusion. The van was stuck, off the driveway and in the mud, as if he was trying to make a U-turn and drive away rather than come back for me. His headlights pointed off into a stand of trees.

"What the fuck, Bob? Were you trying to leave without me? What are you doing?"

"I don't know what I'm doing," he almost whimpered.

Worse, it looked like the van might need a tow. I was in pain and bleeding badly, too crippled to help rock the heavy van out of its rut. I told Bob he had to do the pushing. I took the wheel. After several minutes of stress and strain and spinning wheels, the van was freed. Bob climbed into the passenger seat caked in muck. I drove home one-handed, still gushing blood. The van interior looked like a crime screen.

On the short drive, it occurred to me that after venting thirty years of rage, I had a new problem: *How do I get away with murder?*

First things first—Bob and I had to get our stories straight.

"We gotta talk," I told him.

Bob was near tears. "I just wanna go home and see my little girl." His daughter was three years old.

"Wait here," I said, pulling into my driveway. "I gotta stop this bleeding." I rushed into my house to wrap my wound and stop the bleeding—using a wad of paper towels secured by duct tape. Out the kitchen window, I saw Bob's van backing away. Bob was on the run.

I knew I needed advice. I needed a friend, but I also needed a line of cocaine, a Xanax, a bottle of Ketel One.

And I needed to tell my mother.

Part V

THE ACCUSED

Dreams of getting away with murder were fading faster than I could restore them with drug-induced optimism. I had only hours to craft a cover-up, and I couldn't even count on Bob's help. *The guy ran out on me. Where'd he go?* My convenient excuse for taking vengeance on a very bad man was already getting ping-ponged between my paranoia and my reality checks: *What the hell have I done?* I remembered Paul, my concerned friend from the liquor store. He'd promised to answer his phone if I needed help fighting off Joe Rubino. I called Paul and said only that it was urgent. He showed up within minutes, as did my girlfriend, Cheryl. They helped clean my wound. But they had no suggestions for my much bigger problem: I was about to be wanted for murder. My mind raced. Local doctors might alert police to my suspiciously mangled hand. *How far out of state would I have to run to safely seek emergency treatment with no questions asked? How can I explain all that blood DNA I left at the scene? And the spit? If suicide is my only way out, how will that work? And can I somehow vanish, cease to exist, before morning?* I asked Paul to do one thing: "Please, go upstairs and wake my mother."

Chapter Twenty-Four

GOING BONNIE AND CLYDE

Consider the world of Joan Fredericks as it existed when she went to bed earlier that Tuesday night. She was an eighty-one-year-old widow, mother of three grown children, a grandmother, devout Episcopalian, community volunteer, and do-gooder who counted among her many friends the recently retired sheriff's lieutenant, Boy Scout leader, and American Legion chaplain Dennis Pegg—often a guest in our home over the years.

Then, there was her personable youngest son, the special little boy she had nursed through open-heart surgery before he had even started first grade, now a forty-six-year-old party boy still living at home and, so far, falling short of his professional promise, even as he continued to flounder.

I was, after all, still looking for meaningful work, still unmarried, and—oh, by the way—still hampered in all my pursuits by nearly every addiction known to society.

So, when she was awakened from a sound sleep about midnight—summoned downstairs by a strange voice in the dark saying, "Mrs. Fredericks, Clark needs your help"—my mother was
walking into the shock of her life. No mother could have been
prepared for what was coming. But Joan may have been the least
prepared.

She stepped into our garage and basement apartment area
wearing her robe and nightgown—and froze. I was standing
there covered in blood, calmly self-medicating with a bottle of
Ketel One. All around me was only more blood—it was pooled
on the floor and splattered on walls and cabinets. I had duct tape
rigged around my forearm as a makeshift tourniquet, holding
in place thick folds of once-white paper towels, now oozing red.

Her eyes swept the room, then settled on me. Before she
could ask a question, I answered one: "I just killed Dennis Pegg."

"No! This can't be true. Have you lost your mind?"

"He was a filthy pedophile."

She seemed only more confused. "What? I don't understand
what you're telling me. Why? How? Is it the drugs making you
say this?"

"Mother," I began, trying not to snap back or sound impatient,
"no, this isn't the drugs talking. Pegg's been prancing around this
town for years pretending to be everybody's friend while he mo-
lests kids. He did it for decades. Still was."

Joan's entire world was coming unhinged. She kept shaking
her head and repeating, "No, I can't believe this."

"It had to be done," I insisted. "No one ever did anything. Not
the police. No one! Someone had to stop him."

"You're telling me you *had* to murder Dennis Pegg. But why?"

After all those years—after slitting the man's throat, for God's sake—I was still paralyzed by the shame. I still couldn't tell my mother that Pegg raped me.

I also knew that she had no clue whatsoever about Pegg's past, about the rumors of former jail inmates hitchhiking to get away from Dennis's sleepovers. My father kept his suspicions about Pegg between us. And Mom's women friends, including the Cub Scout den mothers, they all loved Dennis. I finally edged as close to the truth as I dared:

"I did it, Mom, to avenge myself and Jay and Jeff and every other kid in town."

"But why, Clark? Why?" She was pleading more than asking.

I shook my head and tried once more: "I just couldn't lay my head on a pillow another night without thinking about what he was doing to other kids."

"But, Clark!" Now she was sounding impatient. "Why *you*? Why did *you* have to do it?"

Well, she had me there. Her problem was another version of the same question I was already asking myself: *What the hell have you done?* Now, she wanted to know who I thought gave me authority to play Stillwater vigilante.

I shrugged. There was no answer. She finally turned away and slipped silently into Mom mode, gathering rags and soap and a bucket of water. She would spend the rest of the night cleaning up after the bloody mess I'd left—at least so far as soap and water could wipe it away.

I went up to my bed and applied a couple Xanax and more

vodka to the mess in my head, hoping I could figure things out better in the morning. Or wake up dead. If suicide was painless and easy, I would have seriously considered it at that moment. Instead, I switched off my light and went to sleep.

I died only figuratively, sleeping well past sunrise. Thank you, Xanax. In my absence, Mom had not only mopped up the garage, as I would later learn, but had also alerted my sister, Holly—telling her that she needed to come over right away. *What's it about?* Mom wouldn't say over the phone, offering only that "it's something to do with your brother." Once Holly arrived, Mom took her out on the back deck to explain:

"Your brother killed Dennis Pegg last night."

Unbeknownst to me, Holly immediately rushed inside and peeked into my room. She got the confirmation she needed by seeing my duct-taped hand and arm. Mom wanted Holly to help dispose of bags filled with bloody rags from the garage cleanup.

My sister refused. "I'm not going to be an accessory to a crime, Mother!" Holly wanted to know what Joan planned to do next.

"Your brother and I are going to get in the car and drive away."

"Going where?"

"Far." Mom was thinking Florida.

"That's absolutely insane crazy talk! Snap out of it! You're gonna run away with Clark? Go all Bonnie and Clyde on the run? Listen to yourself—you're making no sense."

Like my mother, Holly was also in shock. She didn't want to be there when I woke up. She told Mom she was afraid of me— my temper, my drug use, my dark side. What Holly didn't tell Mom was that she planned to share this new family secret with her personal counselor. Holly was dealing with her own emotional crises at the time—a divorce and a breast cancer diagnosis. Her counselor's name was Diane.

While I slept, and as I would only later learn, Diane urged Holly and our mother to alert state police to conduct a "wellness check" at Pegg's house—just in case Dennis was still alive. If Pegg could be saved, Diane told them, I could be spared capital murder charges. I woke up in time to overhear a version of that proposal suggested to Joan over the phone.

I went ballistic. "No cops! No cops!" I screamed so Holly and Diane could hear it over the phone. I also smacked the furniture with my good fist for emphasis. Holly imagined I was banging my head against a wall. But I knew police doing a wellness check were not going to find Pegg alive.

Still, the counselor kept lobbying Holly and our mother to permit her to send police to Pegg's door. If Dennis was already dead, they reasoned, I might look more sympathetic trying to send help.

Really? The supposedly "sympathetic killer" didn't know that the counselor had already sent police to check on Pegg's "wellness." And, of course, they found a murder scene.

An hour or so later I got my first clue that the secret was out, catching sight of a single uniformed state police officer sneaking into our backyard. His gun was drawn. I poured myself a glass of wine and rushed to another view of the yard from my bedroom window. A second armed officer was taking cover around the corner of our gardening shed. I was about to close the window blinds when we made eye contact.

In that surreal moment, I knew my life was over. I'd got what I'd wished for: I'd woken up dead. There would be no running for out-of-state medical treatment, no cover-ups to construct, no adventures of Bonnie and Clyde with my mother. There was no hope. I was going to jail—and not just any jail. I knew I was going to the same jail that retired sheriff's lieutenant Dennis Pegg once supervised, and into the custody of Pegg's pals and fellow jailers.

I was going to hell.

Chapter Twenty-Five

HE DESERVED IT

M r. Fredericks, come out with your hands up." The order broadcast over a police loudspeaker was intended only for me, but it was heard all over the neighborhood. I knew Mom wasn't going to appreciate that. I didn't know where she had gone, but I figured she was trying to calm the dozen or so heavily armed men out in the yard looking for me. In fact, she had already offered a personal noise complaint to the officer in charge, adding, "What will the neighbors think?"

"Ma'am," he told her, "we don't give a fuck what the neighbors think." He asked her to kindly take a seat in the back of a patrol car.

Meanwhile, a police all-points bulletin had gone out, reporting a homicide and calling for backup at our house. My longtime friend and state trooper Tom Sweatt misunderstood the callout; he thought I must have been the murder *victim*.

"Nope, he's the perp," said the desk officer.

After expressing surprise and disbelief that his friend could be a killer, Tom nonetheless volunteered to stay on duty and join the arrest team. Because of our friendship, he told his boss, "If things go sideways, maybe I can help reason with Clark."

As more police cars arrived, I was taking my time inside— pouring myself a second glass of wine and changing into a clean T-shirt. It had big red letters saying NEW JERSEY STATE POLICE and was a gift from Tom Sweatt a couple of months earlier. By the time I'd changed, Tom was probably one of the officers already out in my yard. Not a surprise. Put a dozen locals together almost anywhere in our small town, including at a police action in my own yard, and I'd easily know a few of them.

The loudspeaker crackled again: "Mr. Fredericks, come out of the house with your hands up."

I chugged my chardonnay, took a long, deep breath, and mumbled aloud my last prayer as a free man: "God, let them shoot me out there. I'm done with life. Take me. Please, God, take me." I unlatched the screen door that stood between me and all those guns and stepped out onto the porch without raising my hands. Instead, I tilted my head back hoping to hear the crack of a gunshot that would put me out of my misery.

It didn't happen. I was ordered onto the lawn, onto my belly, spread-eagled. Then, I was swarmed by officers. Someone wrenched my arms behind my back to handcuff me. I yelped, "Easy on my hand."

Another friend from the arrest team—Don, a plainclothes detective from the county prosecutor's office—ran up to me as I was moved into a sitting position. He was clearly agitated, even distressed:

"Clark! Why, bro? Why? What the fuck?"

"Off-the-record?" I asked, thinking I had to be careful what I told authorities—even if those authorities were friends.

"Sure, sure, off-the-record."

"Pegg was a filthy child molester. He got what was coming to him."

Our exchange was overheard by Tom Sweatt, who stepped close and whispered, "Dude, you gotta keep your mouth shut. Don't say another thing."

Although I very much wanted to be dead, my survival instincts were still engaged. I nodded. Besides, it was easier to simply zone out and count the state police cars.

A few minutes later, Tom was sent into the house "to clear it"—making sure no one else was inside, such as an accomplice or more family members. Then the house would be sealed off until detectives could make a more thorough inspection. Investigators were already preparing a search warrant request.

I wished my ride to the state police station just up the road in Newton could last forever. The views out the squad car windows were all familiar. Near the end, we passed the house I had fixed and flipped for virtually no profit a few years ago, and the Dunkin' Donuts where Mike Funari's mom was harassed and threatened by Dennis Pegg way back when. We passed a Quick-Chek store. This time I didn't think of Pegg so much as I thought of coffee, how they made the best in town, how much I needed a cup that very minute.

No such amenities were offered at the station, known in Newton as the state police barracks. I was shackled to the wall by the wrist above my good right hand and held for what seemed like hours—until the arrival of homicide detective Howard Ryan.

He had just been to Pegg's house, where his examination of the crime scene had already made him one remarkable expert on the murder—and on this murder suspect.

Chapter Twenty-Six

THAT WEIRD GUY

H ey, man—I gotta apologize to you. I'm sorry we didn't stop
him." Those early words from the mouth of New Jersey
State Police detective Howard Ryan almost knocked me over.
Fortunately, I was still sitting on a bench and shackled to the wall.
But I was stunned. *What is this? Some kind of good-cop / bad-cop
setup? Am I supposed to trust this guy?* I just didn't know how to
react. Besides, I was strung out on Xanax, emotionally and physically wasted, and feeling the weight of impending doom. And I
was confused: *Wasn't I supposed to be doing all the confessing?*

"I've heard rumors for a long time," Ryan said of Dennis Pegg.
"Whatever he did to all of you victims, keeping everyone silent,
that's what made it impossible for us to do anything about him.
We can't make cases based on rumors and innuendo."

Ryan had arrived at the Millbrook Road crime scene around
midday to lead the investigation. Here's how the next couple of
hours unfolded, based on the investigator's detailed personal

and public accounts made later to colleagues, journalists, and community groups.

―――

"What have we got here?" he had asked a state police officer escorting him up the long driveway through a wooded area.

"Well," the officer told him, "somebody tried to cut this dude's head off." That was the first clue for this veteran investigator, an insight into the killer's motive and emotional state.

A colleague confirmed it was Dennis Pegg: "This is Pegg's house." That put the crime in a whole new context for Ryan. He had long suspected Pegg of living a double life, of taking inmates home with him. He'd heard rumors of child sex abuse charges being filed against Pegg but later dropped, of potentially incriminating records disappearing.

Those stories made the rounds at local cop hangouts like Kathy's Restaurant, where Pegg was a frequent patron, though he shunned colleagues from law enforcement so obviously that he came to be known by some, including Ryan himself, as "the weird guy."

Ryan wasn't ready to name a suspect so soon after arriving at the crime scene, but he had a powerful hunch that whoever it was, it was probably someone from a list of Pegg's abused victims.

Medical examiners would eventually count more than twenty stab wounds to Pegg's upper body. But what stood out to Ryan were the wounds to his throat. It was cut almost to the bone on both sides. There was blood sprayed on the living room wall. Yet, for all the apparent violence of the attack, the blood was mostly confined to an area immediately around the body. The carpet where he fell resembled a sponge.

To Ryan that also helped narrow the universe of suspects by motive: *This was very personal, not a theft or a robbery. Somebody came in that front door . . . went right to Pegg . . . killed him . . . then left—and that somebody was really, really pissed.*

There was one anomaly. Ryan found a single bloody footprint in the doorway to Pegg's bedroom. *Why would someone covered in blood make a stop in the doorway to the dead man's bedroom?* The mystery bothered Ryan. He made a note about it and finished his inspection.

Soon after, as he left the Pegg house, Ryan encountered a county prosecutor who was also working the scene. The prosecutor shook his head and expressed regrets that such a "brutal" and "horrible tragedy" could have happened in little Sussex County, where homicides of any kind were rare. Ryan had already accepted the likelihood that one of Dennis Pegg's victims had probably killed him.

"It's really not that much of a tragedy," Ryan responded. "You know the rumors about Pegg, don't you? Maybe this is the best reason why you don't rape little kids, because someday they can come back as grown men and cut your head off."

———

Talking to me in my holding cell that same night, Ryan did have some questions. But he made it clear to me that I didn't have to answer them. We were just having a conversation, he said. He was taking no notes and said he had no tape recorder.

First, he wanted to know, whatever it was that Pegg did to me in my life, "Was it a one-time thing or a recurring thing?"

I recoiled. It wasn't that I hated the question so much as I hated myself for the truth behind it. I couldn't make eye contact. I just looked at the floor and said, "It was for years."

"Why now? What made you do it last night?"

I shrugged and thought about that for a moment, then I remembered: "He was still hurting kids. I realized I couldn't go to bed without doing something to stop him."

"One more question. I noticed one bloody footprint in Pegg's bedroom. Why? How did that happen?"

I bowed my head again. I felt my shoulders sag. Was I going to tell this stranger, this cop, what I never told my father, not even on his deathbed? What I didn't tell my mother, not even last night after confessing to murder? What I was still trying to keep buried from my own memory?

But I thought about how much my world had changed, even since Officer Ryan walked into my holding cell. He knew that Pegg was a pedophile. Ryan was already convinced that I was a victim of Pegg's abuse. The state policeman even seemed sympathetic to my motives, for God's sake. The moment had a profoundly Alice-in-Wonderland kind of feel to it—like up was down and down was up. I mean, he was a cop and I was a cop killer. *Was I going to confess to him, of all people?*

"Yes, sir," I finally blurted out. "I only went in far enough to spit on Pegg's bed. The bed where he raped me."

There. I finally said it.

Chapter Twenty-Seven

LIGHTS, CAMERA, KILL ME

Officer Ryan apologized again before leaving the holding cell, advising me that my booking was going to be unpleasant. I would be stripped, searched, photographed, fingerprinted, weighed, and measured. He promised to get some medical attention for my bleeding hand. And he suggested that I spare my mother's house considerable disruption by telling him how to find the murder weapon. I said to look for it in a black garbage bag in the garage. He paused at the door and turned back to me.

"Clark, listen to me. Very soon, homicide detectives are going to take you into another room, and they're gonna question you. You have the right to remain completely silent. I suggest you exercise that right. Keep your mouth shut. Look, this investigation is already over. There are no secrets. Your blood's all over everything. Dennis's blood is all over you. We know whodunit. You're gonna be charged and you're gonna go to jail. But if you go in there and run your mouth, you can only make things worse for yourself. You got it?"

"Yeah." I shrugged and nodded.

"What are you gonna do?" he snapped back at me. It sounded like a test.

"Take the Fifth?"

"Tell them you won't answer any questions without your lawyer."

"What lawyer?"

"I'll take care of it. So, what are you going to say?"

"I'll only talk with my lawyer."

He asked the same question two more times. I answered the same.

And Ryan was gone.

He was right on all counts. My booking was unpleasant. I was taken to an interrogation room where four or five detectives were ready to ask me a lot of questions. I said I was waiting for my attorney.

"That's really how you want to play this?" one of them growled.

"I won't answer any questions without my lawyer." I didn't have to say it again.

I learned later that a noted local defense lawyer—George Daggett, the bane of Sussex County prosecutors for years—had already faxed over to the barracks a formal representation notice. Ryan had made that request in a phone call to Daggett even before he left the barracks, to howls of complaint from his miffed fellow investigators.

Ryan's predictions continued to come true. An ambulance arrived and the medics replaced my wrap of duct tape and paper towels with gauze and bandages and antiseptics. They said I needed emergency surgery for extensive tendon and ligament damage. The hospital called in a hand specialist. I was on an operating table that same evening.

Finally, under the effects of a powerful anesthetic, I went to sleep. A moment later, or so it seemed, I woke up from the combined effects of the anesthetic, an abbreviated recovery period, and a round of strong painkillers.

It was a painful awakening. I was immediately blinded by overhead lighting. Instinctively, I raised both hands to shield my eyes—smacking my face with the heavy plaster cast now covering my left wrist and most of my forearm. *Where did that come from?*

I had only a hazy recollection of being prepped for surgery and an even hazier memory of being transported back to the jail. Based on the darkness I could see beyond my small window to the outside world, I figured it had to be the middle of the night. I might have kept sleeping, but there was no switch to turn off, or even to dim, the ceiling lights, which functioned at this moment like a torture device.

As I looked around the room, the thought of spending the rest of my life in such miserable circumstances was enough to make me nauseous. I tried to suppress it, lying back on the bed. I noticed a camera on the ceiling. Someone must be watching me. *Why?* I sure wasn't going anywhere. The cell door looked to be solid steel except for a small window. I had no recollection of putting on this orange jumpsuit—so ugly it was probably visible in the dark. The floor, covered with hair balls and dust bunnies the size of small tumbleweeds, was especially uninviting in my bare feet. I had neither shoes nor socks.

Now my hands were starting to shake. What I wouldn't give for a line of cocaine or to pop a Xanax or just a shot of vodka. The reality of life without easy access to booze and drugs was beginning to register. I had to fight my panic sensations.

The cell had four walls of graffiti-covered concrete, each wall etched with the scrawled curses, prayers, and philosophies of prior inmates—from SUCK A DICK to I WANT TO DIE. And then there was my favorite: KILL ME. This was no place to bolster anyone's will to live. So, I focused on how to rig my sling as a noose.

An air vent on one wall near the ceiling held potential. The wire-mesh-covered vent with a metal frame was above the toilet and sink, a one-piece stainless-steel contraption that I could stand on to reach it. And since I needed something to do to pass the time, I gave myself a problem to solve:

Is there some way to attach my hospital-issued sling securely enough to that vent to successfully hang myself?

Chapter Twenty-Eight

WHO'S THE MONSTER?

My cell door suddenly swung open, and for the first time I found myself alone with one of my guards. It was a moment of vulnerability that I'd been dreading since it dawned on me: *This is Dennis Pegg's jail.* He had worked here for twenty-eight years, much of it as the supervising officer. So, I was wondering when to expect the beatings. *Now, maybe?*

The guard was brusque, but all business. "The nurse is here," he called out. Then he turned solicitous. "Can you stand and walk?" He seemed ready to assist.

I stood but immediately had to brace myself against the wall. On wobbly legs I stumbled to the open door and into the secured entryway, what the COs (correctional officers) called the sally port. The nurse, a short, grandmotherly type with curly gray hair, was standing beside a medical cart on wheels. At six foot three, I towered over her.

She seemed almost apologetic, asking me to bend down so

she could examine my pupils. Then she did a routine check of my vital signs—pulse, temperature, and heart rate—before examining my left hand in the cast. Her gentle touch and considerate manner seemed so out of place in such an inhumane setting. The comfort I felt caught me by surprise. But the examination wasn't done yet.

"Do you know where you are, Mr. Fredericks?"

I figured this must be some sort of mental acuity test. "I believe it's the county jail."

"You are being held in the camera room. That's to make sure you don't harm yourself. There is no way you should have that sling in there with you. I don't think it's safe, so I'm afraid I will have to ask you to hand it over to me."

I knew the nice nurse was looking out for my own good. But when I handed over the sling, my only hope for a quick end to my nightmare went with it. I had nothing more to look forward to but those jail beatings. The guard motioned me back into my cell. I half expected him to trip me or give me a shove. He just closed the door behind me.

In the hours that followed, my drug-withdrawal symptoms became more noticeable. My legs constantly twitched. My hand throbbed. I couldn't get comfortable. I didn't even have a pillow. *Why would a pillow be banned from the suicide cell?* I couldn't figure that out.

A short time later the cell door opened again. These arrivals were always a surprise; no one knocked or called ahead. I was stretched out on my bed when I heard the door creaking open. My response was instinctively to prep for fight or flight. I quickly swung my feet to the floor. If I had to face some abusive guards, I wanted to see them coming.

But the guy offered a friendly greeting. He looked familiar. "Do you remember me?" His name tag said YANVARY; he was a corporal about my age.

I figured it must have been a work-related contact. "Did I work on your car at my brother's shop in Franklin?"

He shook his head. It turned out Jason Yanvary was a cousin of my childhood best friend, Karl, and when we were kids, the three of us used to ride dirt bikes together. We hadn't seen each other in about thirty years, but back then I was almost a cousin to this correctional officer!

"How are you feeling?"

I told him straight: "Pretty shitty."

He encouraged me to "hang in there," invoking my attacker and victim's name for the first time within the walls of my suicide-prevention cell. "Listen, there are a lot of rumors swirling around about Pegg. Give it time to play out. And don't talk to anybody about anything."

Under the twenty-four-hour light in my cell, I had no idea when a new day began or ended. But I learned quickly that someone was going to open my cell door at least once every eight hours. That's when the guard shifts would change, and a new guy would check in on me.

My next correctional officer was about thirty years old, clean-cut, with dark hair and a friendly smile. "I'm doing a cell check. Is there anything you need?"

This guy sounded more like a concierge than a jailer. I seized the opportunity. "I've got nothing to lay my head on. Am I allowed to have a pillow in the camera room?"

"Sure, I'll get you one. I'll come back just as soon as I finish my rounds."

Now I was really confused. *What is this? I've killed one of their own. Where's the goon squad?* A few minutes later the guy dropped off the pillows. Yes, *two* pillows. I wanted to tip him.

In those first few days, local media weren't sure how to cover the story. The *New Jersey Herald* first called it "an open and shut case, according to prosecutors." Then they carried news that the Historical Society of Stillwater had canceled its weekend strawberry festival due to the death of its former president Dennis Pegg. Another day, police were investigating anonymous reports of new Pegg links to child sex abuse.

My "off-the-record" comment that Pegg got what he deserved had made it into an official police report. And within a week, some national media were reporting about the case, too. United Press International carried a story headline quoting my sister-in-law, Carol, saying that Pegg "molested his accused killer."

I didn't see any of those stories in jail. But friends did, including Anne Marie Hayes, who had married my college roommate. She also had been Lisa Kaufman's roommate when we were all at Northeastern University. I was not surprised to learn later that news of my arrest quickly made the rounds of old friends.

Anne Marie had been the first to tell Lisa. "You need to sit down," she had said in that phone call. "I've got to tell you something before it shows up in *People* magazine." Then she blurted out, "Clark murdered some man who molested him as a boy!"

My college girlfriend, now married, had two sons, nine and thirteen, and lived in New York's Westchester County. She took the revelation with what Anne Marie considered unexpected calm, saying, "Oh, my God. Now I understand."

But I was getting no feedback, no news. Jail was like a black hole those first few days. I had no lawyer yet. And I didn't know that first assistant prosecutor Gregory Mueller had already told reporters that the only mystery in this case was establishing motive and that was where detectives would be focused. It was an investigation within the murder investigation, checking out allegations of Pegg's double life.

Between drop-in visits from various friendly COs, I wrestled with the side effects of withdrawal from my drug addiction, along with the chronic problem of sleeping under bright lights twenty-four hours a day. I think it was Xanax withdrawal that finally sent me into delirium. I began hearing sounds, voices, whole conversations coming from the sally port just outside my door. I would stumble over to the door, look out through its window slot, but never see anyone. Hallucinations followed hallucinations. Untouched food trays came and went as I slipped into and out of incoherence. Time blurred into one long night that lasted more than a week.

Until, finally, it was Sunday—visitors' day at the Sussex County jail, more formally known as the Keogh-Dwyer Correctional Facility. I was escorted out to the visitors' area to meet my mother and sister, Holly. I had not seen them since that morning before my arrest. After more than ten days in jail, I could honestly say that I had never felt such intense loneliness in all my forty-six years.

A wall of windows, partitioned into five semi-private stalls, divided inmates from the visitors they could see but not touch. A phone on each side of the glass connected each inmate to visitors for up to twenty minutes.

During our first few minutes together, no one was able to say a word. One look at those two stricken faces through the glass, and I lost it, bursting into uncontrollable sobbing. I can't explain it. I was so relieved to see them, but also feeling so guilty for causing them so much pain and suffering. We were all a blubbering mess, on both sides of the window.

Mom was first to pick up the telephone handset. She dabbed her eyes, told me she loved me, and put on one of her determined faces. "We're going to get through this, Clark."

Holly seemed especially anxious. When she took her turn on the phone, she blurted out, "I know you hate me, Clark. I am just so very sorry." She had been freaking out that I blamed her for my arrest. Now she hoped I would forgive her for setting in motion the wellness check that led police to discover Pegg's body.

"Holly, I don't hate you," I insisted. "If you hadn't done that, I probably would have killed myself by now. You probably saved my life."

In the minutes we had left before guards called "Time!," we talked about some of the lawyers they had sent to consult with me. I had already interviewed a few of them, meeting in a private room where I spoke over the clanking of my handcuffs on the table as I tried to impress complete strangers with my—what? My innocence? Or, maybe that, murder aside, I was really a nice guy?

The first was a woman who guaranteed she could get me out on bail in three days. Another attorney listed several high-profile clients. I knew most of their cases and couldn't help recalling that all of them had been lost in court.

But Daniel Perez was different. He was the first to tell me, "You have a defensible case." *Really? You mean there might be more to my future than a lifetime of prison cells? Tell me more!*

But Perez also needed more from me than a retainer. He needed to know the truth. It turned into an emotional session for me. He seemed thoughtful and compassionate, so I told him everything.

He was blunt about my situation: I was a suicide risk, he told me. But his concern was about more than simply keeping me safe. It was about protecting my image as a sympathetic defendant. "Forget about bailing out," he said, even if authorities would have considered it, which was unlikely. As a drug addict and an alcoholic and a local party regular, getting out of jail and being seen going to bars and having a good time while awaiting trial for murder, he said, "would be a very bad look."

Plus, every day I spent in my neighborhood jail would be subtracted from any state prison sentence. And he was only too clear about one thing—I was probably going to prison, with or without a defensible case. There was, after all, a dead victim and "horrific crime-scene photos" that would be shared with the jury at trial.

Perez kept telling me facts I didn't want to hear. So I trusted him. He started making a difference on my behalf almost immediately. He pressed police to conduct a second search of Pegg's home, looking for evidence supporting my molestation accusations. He also placed a flurry of other defense motions, including a protective order requesting access to Pegg's computer devices.

A forensics search of those devices would sometime later produce suggestive photos of shirtless young men and boys posing in their underwear.

For all the rumors, Pegg still had many defenders. His former boss, Sussex County sheriff Robert Untig, told reporters Pegg was "a good guy and straight shooter" who always "tried to help people." The president of the Stillwater Historical Society told the *New Jersey Herald* that Pegg was "one of the nicest people you'd ever want to meet . . . an amazing man." Stillwater mayor George Scott said the same and paid tribute to Pegg's extensive volunteer work. And an attorney for Pegg's estate called him "a true giant of Sussex County," dismissing me as a "lowlife" and merely an "alleged child molestation victim."

What I was just coming to realize was that my "alleged molestation"—my deep, dark secret of thirty years—was now getting plastered all over the media. All my neighbors and friends and tire customers and drinking buddies, *everyone* in town now knew my secret, knew I had been sexually abused as a boy.

My niece Kim came in on visitors' day to tell me I was so famous that a local singer-songwriter had written a ballad about me. Its author, Tom Nieman, was singing it from my perspective, with lyrics that told my story. It began with:

Dennis Pegg was a sheriff for the county
He had a badge, a gun, and authority
A pillar of the community. . . .
You shouldn't have done what you did
You were a man and I was just a kid. . . .

Going into my third week, still under those twenty-four-hour-a-day bright lights and a video watch in the suicide cell, I got a visit from CO Shad Steffens. He arrived with his customary big grin, but this time he was bursting with news of his own. "My man!" he greeted me. "You would not believe what's going on in the community. The support you're getting is ridiculous! Somebody's set up a Free Clark website on Facebook. You can order FREE CLARK bumper stickers."

I had a hard time processing Shad's news. It was coming at me so fast and with such enthusiasm I was confused. "You mean I'm not a monster?"

"Not at all. Pegg was the monster. Everyone wants to know why that guy was still walking the streets."

I wanted to hug Shad. I wanted to cry. But he had more to share.

"The word has spread throughout the sheriff's department about what a piece of garbage Pegg was. You should know that we usually wear a blue ribbon when a comrade dies, but none of us have been ordered to do that. Not for Pegg. Not only that, but the flag out front? It's usually flown half-staff for the passing of an officer. Not this time. That should tell you something about how we feel around here about Dennis Pegg."

All I could say was "Wow." I closed my eyes and savored the moment.

I was still a long way from a poll of twelve jurors, but I took some comfort knowing that in a court of public opinion, when judging who's worse, a serial child molester or his killer, it was Pegg who was deemed the monster.

Chapter Twenty-Nine

PRAYERS FOR NUMBER 5

Jail is a natural breeding ground for depression. And even though my circumstances steadily improved, there was no shaking the dismal reality that I was looking at a potential lifetime confined to a cell. I had a hard time sustaining anything close to hope—even with those early reports of community support.

I did finally graduate from the suicide cell though. First stop was an isolation cell, thanks to the cast on my arm. It was considered a potential weapon and, therefore, a threat to others. Then, nearly three months into my new life as a maximum-security prisoner, with that cast removed, I was transferred to the general inmate population.

But I still woke up every morning to a sudden, painfully bright overhead light that went on at precisely 7:00 a.m.—a daily reminder that I was still a prisoner, that I still had no get-out-of-jail date, and that this was going to be my life as far as I could see. While I hated pretty much everything about my days

in custody, that jolting 7:00 a.m. blast of light came to represent
the worst of it all.

Landing Dan Perez as my defense counsel gave an immediate boost to my morale, but he came with a steady supply of
reality checks, too. After all, we still had to prove that I was a
child victim of Pegg's sex abuse. There were no living witnesses.
And remember, I never told anyone. Not my closest friends. Not
even my dad when he asked me point-blank. Rumors about Pegg
might be helpful, but they were unlikely to be presented in court
without real, live eyewitnesses to Pegg's improper conduct. And
since Dan could not argue that I was innocent, his only option
was to make a case for some form of diminished capacity so as
to chip away at the severity of my sentence. Dan said he didn't
have to prove that I was temporarily insane—only that my judgment was impaired. The legal term was *passion provocation*.
Passion provocation was no slam-dunk, either, especially given
that great gap of time between my being raped and losing my
mind at Pegg's door some thirty-five years later.

The range of sentencing possibilities was broad, too, topping
out at life in prison. That ultimate penalty weighed on my mind
every day. It was like playing Russian roulette and imagining the
bullet in every chamber. Dan was optimistic about getting something more moderate—say, around ten years, with a chance to
nudge actual prison time lower with a record of good behavior.
I appreciated the difference between a life term and a decade or
so. But it didn't make me, what can I say—happy?

So I found comfort where I could, in junk food—jailhouse
commissary favorites like the Whole Shabang potato chips and

Smartfood white cheddar popcorn. Bag after bag of them. Candy bars, crackers, cookies, tons of sweets of all kinds. That's what got me through most of those early days. My strategy was to eat my sorrows away.

One advantage of being in the general population was access to a few—very few—self-improvement programs. A woman from Alcoholics Anonymous, for instance, came in to lead a daily hour of what was known as sharing and confessing. My lawyer thought that was a bad idea. A second option was a Catholic religious service, offering a version of daily mass. The only other program was an evening Bible study group. I considered it, but I still harbored an aversion to prayer. I couldn't do it.

Not since the rape, not since I was twelve years old, could I close my eyes and imagine talking to God without experiencing the rape all over again—reexperiencing the betrayal, my shock and disappointment, my anger with God for failing me. My aversion to prayer had only gotten worse in jail. Now, closing my eyes to pray conjured up competing images of that old sexual attack interspersed with new scenes from the murder—Pegg fighting me off, the blood everywhere, my rage, his fear, his dead eyes.

To me, prayer meant wide-awake nightmares. *Maybe I don't have to actually pray,* I thought. But Bible study wasn't what I wanted at all. What I really, urgently wanted was a line of cocaine and a glass of red wine. But Bible study did offer an hour away from my cell. So, reluctantly, I signed up.

It took a couple of elevator runs to transfer more than a dozen of us inmates down to a second-floor room off the visitors' area. Chairs were arranged there, as if for a lecture, where Brother

Bob would talk to us about the Bible. I didn't know him, had never heard of him. He was an assistant pastor from the Christian Faith Fellowship Church in nearby Hardyston Township.

I arrived ready to change my mind, hanging back, sitting in the last row where I could call the guards to get me the hell outta there if necessary. Brother Bob greeted each inmate with a handshake or a hug. I was last. He put an arm around me and whispered in my ear, "I've been praying for you. So has my congregation."

"You know who I am?" I was startled and pulled back to see he was smiling.

"I do. I prepared this talk when I heard you were coming."

I wasn't sure what to say except "Wow. Thanks."

Brother Bob began his talk with a prayer. I kept my eyes open. Then he introduced his lesson for the evening, the notion that God created man with free will. Man chooses to do good or evil. God is not a puppet master who makes anyone do or not do what's right or good or moral. Good things and bad things happen to everyone. We are judged by how we deal with the good and the bad. People use their free will to make their own choices; God doesn't do it for us, or to us.

Former *altar-boy me* was hearing all this for the first time. I took it to mean that it had been Dennis Pegg's *choice* to rape me. It wasn't God's plan for me. It was the pedophile's free will in action. Brother Bob was giving me permission to stop blaming God for my abuse. When he ended his Bible lesson with a prayer, I closed my eyes—and for once saw only the friendly face of Brother Bob.

Sometime in the next two or three weeks, as I talked to my mother through the glass during Sunday visiting hours, she was excited to tell me about her encounter outside the jail with her minister from the nearby Episcopal church.

"He was coming out of the jail as I was waiting in line to come in," she said. "He came over and gave me a hug, then took me by both shoulders and said, 'Joan, I want you and your son to start praying on the number five, as in a five-year sentence.'" The minister had just had a conversation with some lieutenant in the jail, who told him five years was the lowest sentence possible for a murder conviction in New Jersey.

Dan Perez had never mentioned such a possibility, so I thought it best to humor her. I laughed and told her that she had to pick a more realistic number, that not even God could pull off such a miracle. But she wasn't in a joking mood and snapped right back at me, "I believe in God. I believe in miracles. And I want you to start believing, too."

I felt so bad about what she was going through because of me, so I nodded and assured her I would do just that. The next morning my cell lights roused me from a dead sleep again at 7:00 a.m. Another day of tedium and fear and depression was coming. I had a very different prayer in mind: *God, you've got to help me, either to kill myself or to heal myself.*

Chapter Thirty

SLOW SUICIDE

No booming voice from heaven offered me immediate advice, but as I surveyed my cell stacked with books from friends and strangers, I knew there had to be a lot of wisdom waiting in those pages. *Maybe God wants me to read.* The first book I opened that morning was *Man's Search for Meaning.* I wasn't looking for that title, and I wasn't looking for meaning in my life—not beyond counting how many times that miserable ceiling light went off at 7:00 a.m.

But something about the author caught my attention. Viktor Frankl, a Jewish psychiatrist in Austria, had survived years in Nazi death camps. I figured he had unique authority to advise me on how to deal with incarceration. His advice was to find meaning in life by doing something significant and finding meaning in suffering by showing courage. Frankl's message could be summed up simply: when faced with a situation you cannot change, you are challenged to change yourself. It spoke to me, so I made a deal with God. *All right, Lord, I'm gonna read this one.*

It didn't cure me of depression. Neither was it immediately apparent how I could cure myself or find meaning in my wasted life. But it did give me something to think about, something more positive than how to kill myself. Meanwhile, I kept scarfing down chips and popcorn and candy bars, treating my depression with sugar and salt while losing myself in books and stories that exercised my mind. What I did not exercise was the rest of me.

Well, with one exception. The jail medical advisers arranged for a physical therapist to visit and work with me to regain strength and flexibility in my repaired left hand. That meant a daily regimen of hand exercises—squeezing a tennis ball or a fistful of Play-Doh for twenty minutes at a time.

On the legal front, a series of developments gave me moments of hope that I might even win acquittal. In one case, a woman told police in another county that Pegg had accepted sexual favors from her boyfriend in exchange for reducing the man's jail time in Sussex County on a drunk-driving conviction. Under the Sheriff's Labor Assistance Program (SLAP), which allowed prisoners to work off jail time by doing road cleanup work, the boyfriend had instead provided sexual favors to the Sussex County sheriff's lieutenant.

In her statement to Warren County detectives, the woman said she drove her friend to Pegg's Millbrook Road home "quite a few times" after the boyfriend was released from the Sussex County jail with a revoked driver's license. Her disclosure served our defense strategy "to put Dennis Pegg on trial." At the same time, several grown child-victims of Pegg's—most of them anonymous or unwilling to testify on the record—continued to come forward, at least reinforcing the credibility of my claims against him.

But the disclosure that made the biggest news came from my old classmate Mike Funari. On a Sunday morning in October, Mike's name and photograph showed up along with Pegg's in the *Star-Ledger*, New Jersey's biggest newspaper, with his account of how Pegg groomed and molested him. The sex abuse charges against Pegg that Mike and his mother filed, and later withdrew out of fear of Pegg, were ultimately confirmed by authorities—although a paper record was never found.

According to Mike's account, Pegg had plied him with alcohol and showed him naked pictures that included children having sex. He said Pegg molested him over a period of two years, beginning when he was thirteen years old and had been hired to mow the man's yard. In the story, Funari called a secluded path he took to Pegg's house "the molestation trail."

Dan Perez called that press account "all we need" to corroborate the same pattern of grooming and abuse that I had experienced. He did not, however, encourage me to dream of an acquittal, reminding me of an inconvenient fact: "There's that dead guy in the living room." I had been formally charged with a homicide in the first degree. Even if everything I said was true, he explained, a jury might not excuse it as grounds for deadly violence—especially decades after the abuse.

About that thirty-year gap in my case: the five-year statute of limitations in New Jersey meant that on the day I killed Pegg,

I had no recourse under the law to file a criminal complaint against him for what he did to me as a kid. That was crazy. How could anyone expect children to report sex crimes against them within five years, when they're still too terrified or ashamed to tell their own parents?

For now, I focused on the only source of entertainment that could ease my endless boredom—books. Besides Frankl and the Bible, I had novels and nonfiction, spiritual books and books on meditation, inspirational and self-help books—usually keeping three or four books going at any one time. And I had my chips and cheddar popcorn and cookies and candy bars. That's what got me through so many long days in my cell.

It was taking a toll on my body, though; my weight gain was becoming a concern to the jail medical staff. I was up about sixty pounds since I'd checked into my suicide cell months before. The nurse practitioner knew about my childhood heart condition. She poked and prodded my ballooning arms and legs, worried that it was a possible sign of impending heart failure. She talked about edema.

I suspect she was most concerned that I might die on her watch and set off a nasty inquiry—you know, like "Who killed Clark Fredericks in Dennis Pegg's jail?" I insisted that I felt fine. Unfortunately, as a more direct way out of my troubles, eating myself to death was likely to be the slowest of all forms of suicide.

Enter Dan Perez, hitting me with another unwelcome truth: "Jesus, Clark! You're fat. Looks like you've eaten the whole jail!" As usual, blunt-spoken Dan was looking out for my best interests: "I gotta have you healthy."

The jail staff arranged for me to be examined by a cardiologist. I entered the waiting room of a Newton doctor escorted by two sheriff's deputies, handcuffed and hobbled and decked out in my jailhouse jumpsuit. I shuffled in looking like an orange penguin.

I couldn't help thinking my arrival in this room full of elderly cardiac patients risked setting off every pacemaker alarm in the house. Almost immediately a nurse rushed us off to an empty examination room to check my heart and blood pressure. They were fine. It was my eating habits and sedentary life that threatened my health.

Also, my body seemed to be deteriorating. Everything was starting to hurt—my back, my legs, my knees. I was having constant stomachaches and pains. I was going out to the jailhouse nurse three times a day for a hit of Maalox. In body and mind, I was in trouble. And since my incarceration wasn't going to end anytime soon, I had only one option: the challenge to change myself—body and mind.

Alone in my cell, I dropped to the floor determined to do a couple sets of push-ups. I struggled to complete two push-ups. So much for my past life as the Arnold Schwarzenegger of New Jersey. Now, I was just an overweight wimp.

Chapter Thirty-One

LAST HUGS

C onversations between the defense and the prosecution about my appropriate punishment had begun within weeks of my arrest. From the beginning, Dan Perez cautioned me to keep my hopes and expectations in check. Prosecutor Greg Mueller was under pressure to hold tight on charging first-degree murder. Others in the district attorney's office were adamant: "No deals. Let a jury decide." That seemed fine with me. Even a long-shot acquittal was worth a try. Besides, I wanted my day in court to tell the world that Pegg was a scumbag to me and to a lot of other boys.

Facing first-degree murder charges was risky, Dan cautioned. But the final decision would be mine to make, he said.

On the other side, first assistant prosecutor Mueller seemed to be not nearly as confident of conviction as his "No deals" colleagues. In one early hearing before Judge Thomas Critchley, the prosecutor complained about all the FREE CLARK bumper stickers he saw on his way to court. It seemed to him that "every pickup truck" in Newton had one. Officially, he was concerned about impaneling an impartial jury amid such a widespread community response. He would later confess that what he most dreaded was endless hung juries, or even an acquittal.

In a series of candid discussions, Dan and Greg compared notes on the evidence—what worked for our defense and what worked against us based on the same evidence. Child sexual abuse evidence favoring the defense was circumstantial but powerfully corroborated by the Funari family and by law enforcement confirmation of the complaint the family filed in the early 1980s. Horrific crime-scene photos that might seem to favor the prosecution also supported the defense narrative of passion provocation and diminished capacity.

Defense and prosecution agreed on one thing from the start: there was "compelling evidence on both sides." A legal conundrum, this was a textbook example of a case ripe for a plea deal.

Dan had even more reasons why we might be better off avoiding trial. First, he wanted me to be aware of the practical implications of his own nonscientific sampling of public opinion, something he had noticed in talking about my by-then famous case with random people around town. He called his results "gross stereotyping," but he had found men and women reacted in different ways to my story—something so predictable that it was likely to influence his jury selection priorities if we went to trial.

While both genders tended to be equally sympathetic toward me as a victim of abuse, men tended to view Pegg most harshly.

Typical from men was "He deserved what he got" and "Clark did the community a favor" and "I hope I'm on Clark's jury so I can cut him loose." Women, by contrast and by a wide margin, tended to support Clark with a "Yes, but—you can't take the law into your own hands" and "Yes, but—he shouldn't have killed the man" and "Yes, but—that doesn't justify murder."

Dan warned me, "If we end up with a lot of women on our jury, I think we stand the very real possibility of having a sympathetic jury that still delivers a murder conviction."

Second, Dan played the mom card on me. He started by pointing out that murder convictions come with minimum sentences, which meant that if I went to trial and was convicted of murder, I could count on a decade in prison. My mother could be well into her nineties before my release.

In effect, he was asking me, Was it worth going for an iffy acquittal if failure likely doomed me to prison for the rest of my mother's life?

It wasn't a choice facing me—yet. A plea deal was nothing more than a conversation, so far. Meanwhile, I could see my mother once a week through the glass on Sunday visitors' day. We caught up over the scratchy phone connection, where her first question was usually "How are you doing?" I was always "fine." But without the reassuring hugs we were used to sharing, no conversation was ever complete.

Heading into the New Year of 2013, I wanted to change that. I wanted to put my arm around my mother. I wanted some quality, not-through-the-window time with Mom. One of the Sussex County undersheriffs responsible for the jail was also a Fredericks family friend of long-standing. One day he asked how I was getting along, and I seized the moment. I told him how much my mother was suffering: "This is killing her. It would mean a lot if we could visit in private."

The jail did not permit what it called "contact visits" with max security inmates like me. But within another month or so, the undersheriff made an exception. My mother and I were allowed to meet in the Bible study area on the second floor. I was sitting there when she was escorted in by a guard. I stood and wrapped her in a big hug.

It lasted only seconds until the guard called out, "All right, Fredericks, take a seat—and leave one chair between you." He stepped back against the wall but remained close enough to hear our entire conversation. As usual, Mom just wanted to know how I was doing. "And don't sugarcoat it," she said.

"I'm fine, really," I said, but then I proceeded to sugarcoat it. Our time together flew by.

"Five minutes, Fredericks," announced the guard.

Then, time was up. Mom reached for my hand.

I asked for permission: "Can I give her another hug?"

The guard nodded. We got a few more seconds holding each other. I felt better. I didn't know it would be our last hug for nearly five years.

Chapter Thirty-Two

MY HERO

Inmate housing at the Sussex County jail was concentrated in a five-story tower divided into tiers of cells. My home was on the fifth level—5R-T (5 Right-Top). There was a 5R-B for the bottom tier, reached by an open stairway. Each tier, top and bottom, had its own showers and bathrooms. There were also common-area pay phones, a wall-mounted television, sitting areas, a picnic table, and a window on the outside world. A glassed-in guard station called the Bubble divided both left and right tiers.

Five Left was reserved for inmates considered at risk, a sort of jailhouse equivalent to the witness protection program—for targets of bullying, for instance. Specifically, inmates accused of child molesting were not supposed to be housed in 5R in the company of a murder suspect that had killed his molester. Yeah, it was to protect them from me. I considered it more of a molester protection program.

Sometimes that separation plan failed. A clerical error, they called it. My paranoid side wondered if I was being set up, to be provoked into fighting some scumbag, just enough for me to get hit with some kind of assault-and-battery charge—and extra jail time. A guard would sometimes take me aside to whisper that this guy or that dude is "a kiddie toucher."

The first time it happened, I told the kiddie toucher that he had to leave. He protested, "I'm not in here for that. You got the wrong dude."

All I could do was shrug and apologize. "If we've got the wrong information, I apologize. But otherwise, you gotta hit the buzzer, or you've got a problem." He thought about it for about thirty seconds.

"The buzzer" was near the door to our tier. In cases of emergency or any urgent concern, hitting the buzzer put an inmate in immediate voice contact with guards. The kiddie toucher did just that. "What do you want?" he was asked. After some confusion over what precisely he needed, the inmate blurted out, "Protective custody."

Another time, an accused pedophile was assigned to my cell and had spent a couple of days as my "bunkie" before the guards ratted him out. In that instance, inmate Steve delivered the ultimatum. Steve was the 5R tier enforcer, known for keeping the peace by physical force as required. We called it "body work."

My new cellmate complained, "Why do I have to move? Clark's a cool dude."

Steve was always blunt with the pedos: "Hit the buzzer, or you might never walk again."

I admired Steve, but his style wasn't mine. As part of the *new me* or, at least, the *changing me*, I focused on kindness. I became the helpful guy, sharing my commissary treats with new arrivals. Most of them were jailed on drug-related charges. Even those with burglary or robbery allegations were likely to have committed those crimes to buy drugs. Most were heroin addicts, suddenly desperate for sugar and caffeine—candy and coffee.

My local celebrity status, with lots of friends and family in the neighborhood, meant that I always had a generous balance from donations to my commissary account. I used it to help other guys get necessities, too—like extra socks and underwear. I hadn't exactly found meaning in my life, but I liked the way I felt about myself, offering simple kindness in this cold and hostile place. It lifted my spirits. So, I did it mostly for me—with thanks to Viktor Frankl and Brother Bob.

One day, a few months into my jail stay, I was sitting alone on the tier just looking out the window when a guy sat down uninvited next to me on my bench. Inmates learn early to trust no one—to avoid small talk and to never speak about your case with anyone but your lawyer.

"What's up?" I said in my most suspicious and unwelcoming tone.

"Look, I don't want to talk about your case. I just want to say, from what I read in the papers—the same thing happened to me. It drove me to heroin."

I understood. "Sorry, dude" was all I could say.

"Yeah, I just wanted you to know that I stand behind you one hundred percent."

Another time, a new guy on the tier came up to me with his hand out offering to shake mine. That's another thing you don't do in jail. Maybe a fist bump between buddies. But no handshakes between strangers. It can make you vulnerable. I was wary, but I shook it.

"I just got off the phone with my brother," the guy said. "We used to mow the grass for Dennis Pegg—back when we were ten and eleven years old. A couple times when I couldn't go along on the job, Pegg got him drunk and did stuff."

The guy said his older brother was now a heroin addict and his life "a complete mess, but he wanted me to thank you for both of us for what you've done."

And at the courthouse where a group of us were waiting in holding cells for separate hearings, a woman called out to me asking if I was Clark Fredericks. I confessed I was. She said she, too, was molested as a child. "You're my hero," she told me.

I never knew how to take such gestures of approval. I mean, how could I rationalize compliments and gratitude for conduct that the State of New Jersey could use to toss me into prison for the rest of my life?

A key step down the road toward a more favorable plea deal came nearly a year into custody. My attorney arranged for my psychological evaluation. This would not be some dating-site compatibility test. At stake were years of freedom versus years of prison. My evaluator was a forensics psychologist named Dawn M. Hughes from New York City.

Dan Perez told me with his typical bluntness, "Tell her absolutely everything." By that, he meant everything that had got me a room in 5R-T. Everything that had brought me pain, shame, guilt, and fear. Everything that had made me a victim, and a killer. All the details. "Leave nothing out," he emphasized. "Be completely honest."

Complete honesty was the opposite of my greatest life skill, keeping my secrets buried.

I was escorted to the first-floor visitors' area to wait for Dr. Hughes outside one of the small attorney conference rooms. Calling it "a room" was being generous. It was probably eight feet by eight feet, just big enough for a small table and two chairs— but it felt even smaller. By comparison, my cell was spacious. Waiting to meet with a stranger in that confined space, to tell her the whole story of my rape—every degrading, humiliating, and shameful detail—flooded my mind with images of Pegg's house and sensations of feeling trapped.

And here I was, trapped again. Throughout my life I had fled such situations. To avoid feeling trapped I had sabotaged my career options, sabotaged romantic commitments, disappeared into drug and alcohol fogs. I wanted to run. Instead, I broke into a cold sweat and was having trouble breathing. I had to focus on taking deep breaths and slowly exhaling, trying to calm myself.

By the time she arrived I was well into my panic attack. This would be only the second time I told my story to anyone. It only added to my discomfort having to tell it to a woman. Somehow baring my emotional nakedness to a woman seemed different. My anxieties only grew. And that was without the added stress and worry over the legal implications of what we would be discussing across that table.

Dan said to tell her everything. But what if I say the wrong thing? There must be wrong things to say. And what if she doesn't believe me? What if she thinks I'm a public menace and should stay in prison, maybe for life?

Chapter Thirty-Three

JAILHOUSE GURU

It was everything I dreaded, a five-hour ordeal of remembering the worst days of my life. Dr. Hughes was pleasant, about my age, patient but prodding. "Take your time," she would say when I dissolved into spasms of uncontrollable sobs. Or when I choked up so badly that my words came out as unintelligible squeaks. Yeah, I was a hot mess. And no wonder. As she put it later—and here I translate from her original clinical terms—*Victims who have kept secret the details of their abuse are far more likely to suffer the most severe traumatic-stress symptoms.*

That was me. Going into that first session, however, I was still trying to give her the bare minimum of my story. And she knew it. She insisted on probing beyond the factual details, asking how I felt about this that happened to *eleven-year-old me* and about that when it happened to *twelve-year-old me*—the very things that I had buried the deepest in my psyche. As it turns out, a whole science has developed around the psychological damage to childhood victims of sexual abuse. And I thought it only happened to me.

Through the spring and summer of 2013, Dawn Hughes and I spent fifteen hours together across three separate sessions exploring my memories and emotions. Yes, it got easier. But there were also lots of tests—among them the MMSE (formally, the Mini Mental State Exam). It confirmed I didn't have dementia. The M-FAST (the Miller Forensic Assessment of Symptoms Test) confirmed that I wasn't faking it and that I was, as she would conclude, severely and chronically depressed. The Personality Assessment Inventory produced more evidence not only of depression but also of "anxiety, tension, stress . . . and suicidality," whatever that is.

These tests took hours, with hundreds of questions that ranged from multiple choice to yes-or-no to "check whatever statement applies to you," including this nugget straight out of my first pre-meeting panic attack: "I get physical reactions to reminders of abuse experiences, breaking out in cold sweat . . . trouble breathing . . . etc."

In her summary Dr. Hughes concluded that "after a trauma, the brain needs to both remember and forget. Forgetting allows for new learning to occur. Unfortunately, severe trauma may not let the individual forget." In my case, she said, I continued "reliving this trauma in varying degrees of intensity" for my entire life. While I had been successful burying those trauma memories for many years, by the night of June 12, 2012, I could no longer cope with "the psychologically overwhelming and debilitating experience of remembering."

She described my bursting into Dennis Pegg's house that night in clinical terms, saying that my thinking and cognitive processes were being "mediated and governed" by my traumatized state of mind.

Dan Perez considered the report useful for our defense. The final version wasn't ready for submission to the prosecution until more than a year and a half later, in the spring of 2015. Meanwhile, I was racking up jail time close to home. My friends and family could visit me every Sunday, and lawyer Dan was only a six-minute walk from the visitors' floor.

He was in no hurry to rush Greg Mueller's plea deal offer. If we ended up going to trial, Dan was more than content to have me building up hours in custody. Even a sympathetic jury might want to assess some measure of punishment to discourage any form of vigilante justice. So, by the time my psych evaluation landed in the Sussex County district attorney's office, I was nearing the three-year anniversary of my arrest. I guess it only felt like an eternity to me.

Meanwhile, having been unable, in the words of Viktor Frankl, to change my circumstances at the Keogh-Dwyer Correctional Facility, I was getting well along in changing myself. My exercise regimen had expanded to include yoga and meditation. Now, instead of struggling to do two push-ups at a time, I was doing two hundred, plus sit-ups and other strength builders. I used a walking track around a portion of the first-floor roof as part of my daily aerobic workout. I had also petitioned the commissary to carry more protein foods, including beef jerky, and my sweets had been replaced by boiled eggs that I accumulated in trades for candy with fellow inmates. Those sixty pounds I gained during my first year had been trimmed in half.

I was still sharing plenty of coffee and sweets with the steady flow of heroin addicts that seemed to dominate our community of the incarcerated. Many of them ended up transferred to a nearby drug rehab facility—Sunrise House—where my ex-girlfriend Jaime worked. I told the guys to say hi for me. Sometimes I'd talk to Jaime on the jail phone and ask her to look out for a particular inmate.

"You know, Clark, you're a popular guy over there," she told me one day on the phone. I just laughed. I was still trying to spread around acts of kindness. Besides my little "welcome wagon" of coffee for the newcomers, I had started helping others write letters to their lawyers or to probation officers.

One Spanish-speaking guy with an Anglo girlfriend had me compose his English love letter urging her to wait for him. He was facing ten years for selling drugs. Other guys needed help crafting their allocutions—where they tell the judge that they're guilty but asking for mercy in his sentencing. They would describe their cases to me, and I'd write a page or two admitting that they did the crime but also expressing their remorse. I considered the favors part of my personal kindness campaign, my contribution to making jail a little more bearable.

But I was still surprised by Jaime's description of my popularity on the 5R tier. I asked her, "How do you know?"

"They even have a nickname for you. You're the Jailhouse Guru."

Chapter Thirty-Four

THE DEAL

O n the morning of the night that I killed Dennis Pegg—the morning that I turned on my television set at home in Stillwater and saw pedophile defendant Jerry Sandusky outside court arriving for his sex abuse trial, the morning that I exploded in fury when news cameras caught Sandusky's confident smirk—yeah, that same *damned smirk*—on that same morning first assistant prosecutor Gregory Mueller was watching, too. He remembered that smirk when he saw it cited in my psych evaluation, one of the triggering events that led me to Pegg's front door that night.

"Yeah, I saw that myself—Sandusky with that smirk on his face," he told an interviewer. "He seemed so sure he was going to beat it."

And by the time my psych report landed on Mueller's desk in April 2015—nearly three years after my arrest—the prosecutor also knew from his extensive investigation that a lot more victims of Pegg's criminal conduct were out there in the world than just Clark Fredericks.

Some of those victims had come forward voluntarily and on the record, some anonymously. One suicide victim was likely another victim. Six months earlier, one of Pegg's nephews shot himself to death after being questioned by detectives. His picture in a suggestive pose had been found among similar images of other boys and young men recovered from his uncle's personal computer.

By that time Mueller also knew that state police had confirmed newspaper accounts of the Mike Funari story, that the boy and his mother had filed child sex abuse charges against Pegg back around 1980. Even some of Pegg's friends had provided detectives with leads to broaden their investigation. One friend had acknowledged what he described to investigators as a certain "creep factor" in describing Pegg's fondness for Boy Scouts.

So, my lead prosecutor already had his own serious suspicions about Pegg. Still, he was under pressure from colleagues in his own office to be aggressive—to charge me with first-degree murder "and let a jury decide."

The problem for Mueller was that so many of the possible outcomes didn't feel like justice. A murder conviction would mean a thirty-years-to-life sentence for someone like me with no criminal record who was raped by the murdered man, while the risk of an acquittal could sanction vigilante justice.

In conversations over the months between my prosecutor and my defense lawyer, the two of them searched for common ground. They looked for examples of murder cases being defended on the grounds of passion provocation. Most typically, that defense applied to a defendant who reacted in the moment, under stress, without cool consideration of the consequences. The textbook example: catching a spouse in bed with a stranger.

But a murder committed some thirty years after the trauma occurred? That case seemed never to have made it into a court-room before. So, like a couple of law school students in moot court, Mueller and Perez went back and forth weighing the strengths and weaknesses of each other's case, even as they ne-gotiated options for a plea agreement.

Until the state's own forensics psychologist sided with the de-fense. Dr. Louis Schlesinger agreed with Dr. Dawn Hughes that trauma damage can be triggered long after the injury was suf-fered. And damage from such an injury, left untreated, can last a lifetime. You might say, as evidence of that argument, I was exhibit A.

And that's when Mueller started drafting his proposed plea agreement. I hadn't seen it yet, but within days of my third anni-versary as an inmate facing a life sentence, I dared to hope for a future in freedom. Maybe God could even deliver on my prayers for the number 5.

On June 1, 2015, Dan Perez sent me Greg Mueller's proposal. If I would agree to plead guilty, the State of New Jersey would reduce my charges to second-degree manslaughter and recom-mend prison time not to exceed ten years. Dan said that sentenc-ing was most likely in an official range of five to ten years. What he didn't share was that Judge Critchley had already said in a private conference with the lawyers that he was likely to impose no more than seven years, subject to a formal pre-sentencing hearing still to be held.

I recommend that you take this deal, Dan told me in the note he attached to six pages of forms I would have to fill out, sign, and date. The gravity of that moment made me stop and think— I was about to eliminate the risk of a life sentence, but that also meant no trial and no long-shot chance for acquittal. Deep down I still wanted that trial, if only to hammer Dennis Pegg, to show who this so-called pillar of the community really was.

But the plea deal accommodated that, too—promising an extended pre-sentencing hearing where I would be allowed to tell my story in my own words in an allocution of my own. I could speak in open court and on the record confessing to killing Pegg—but also explaining why I did it.

Dan asked me not to talk with anyone about our pending— but still secret—agreement. *Please keep this close to the vest,* he said in his note of recommendation. *We have been successful keeping the lid on this case press-wise for a while and would like to keep it that way for now.*

It was clear to me that my own attorney considered this offer extremely favorable to our side. He just didn't want to risk word leaking out and turning into headlines and those turning into possible complaints about a slap on the wrist for a killer. The last thing we needed was to invite a last-minute pressure campaign on Mueller from critics among his colleagues on the inside or from Pegg's friends or others out in the public.

I told no one, immediately signed the plea form, and went to work writing my allocution.

Dan provided the yellow legal pad, and the jail commissary had plenty of "security pens" like the ones I used to write letters for fellow inmates. They were flexible, four-inch pens that could not be crafted into jailhouse weapons. I threw myself into scrawling eleven pages of angry prose before showing the tirade to my lawyer.

He rejected page after page with big Xs and advised me to "try a more positive message—what have you learned that can help others—tell them how your silence hurts you." This went on and on through three revisions and some fine-tuning until Dan declared, "That's pretty good."

A couple of weeks after the plea deal had been okayed by all sides, I was summoned from my cell for the long walk from the jail through a cavernous underground tunnel linking it to the courthouse. The walk was particularly slow since my ankles were shackled, as well as my hands and arms. The result is an awkward gait known to us all as "the penguin walk." A pair of jail guards accompanied me throughout the plodding and clanking transit, one at each elbow, to keep me from tripping and falling over my chains.

By now, the reality of some kind of plea deal was the talk of the 5R tier. All the guards, many of them friends now, knew that I would be making a statement and entering a plea in court that day. And whatever happened at a future sentencing hearing, I was no longer looking at life in prison. Both of my escorts were excited about the good news and chatted away with encouragement and good wishes and regrets they couldn't stay to catch my show. Or at least that's what I gathered. The truth is I heard almost none of it. My mind was a million miles away. I was about to tell a courtroom full of family and friends the details of my abuse—all but my lawyer hearing most of it for the first time.

It had been tough enough doing this alone with Dan Perez or Dr. Hughes. But now I was imagining all those eyes on me in a big, brightly lit courtroom. My mom would be there with Holly and Jay, an especially sensitive audience for me. I was about to mention my brother as one of Pegg's victims—not by name, only as a "close relative." But everyone who knew our family would know I was talking about Jay. And I was going to tie our friend Jeff's suicide to Pegg. Not in a whisper, but for the record and transcribed by a court stenographer.

It was about to be oh, so very, very public.

At the end of our underground walk, my escorts got me to the courthouse elevator and said, "Good luck, man." Courthouse guards took me from there to a holding cell a few steps outside Judge Critchley's chambers.

Immediately, I was having trouble breathing again. I focused on deep breaths and slowly exhaling. I prayed for strength. I prayed not to pass out. I tried meditation. I focused on breathing again. And I waited, alone with my thoughts and prayers. Where was Dan? I had expected my lawyer for a brief meeting before facing the court.

Finally, guards entered the holding cell to move me, but I still wasn't going into court. They were shifting me over to a cramped steel-mesh cage where prisoners could meet alone with their lawyers.

Dan was there. "There's been a delay," he said. "Another fifteen to twenty minutes, a half hour max." The problem, he explained, was the crowd.

The crowd?

"Yeah, the place is packed. It's a madhouse. Every news channel's out there, setting up to record. There are cameras everywhere, and overflow crowds out in the hallway, and down the courthouse steps."

What?

That was not what I needed to hear at that moment. I spent the next eternity back in the holding cell praying and trying to breathe and trying not to count the minutes.

Chapter Thirty-Five

WELL, THAT'S A FIRST

J udge Critchley's court was my home away from home at the far end of the tunnel linking jailhouse to courthouse. Most of my hearings had been there through my three-year residency as an inmate awaiting trial, most of them without more than a handful of onlookers. Now I was bracing myself for a very different scene. I took one more deep breath as guards pushed open the courtroom door allowing me to shuffle into what Dan had just called "a madhouse."

It was packed with visitors, but it was also quiet and peaceful. Almost spooky. The only sounds were my chains rattling. At second glance, it also seemed that the entire crowd was familiar faces—friends, family, former college roommates. And every face was frozen in what I imagined was the same mask of tension that I was wearing.

I immediately recognized Rose Funari in the seat nearest to the door. She was the sister of Mike Funari, part of the unofficial "family" of Pegg victims. Next along those prime front-row seats was my brother, Jay, and his daughter, Kim, then my sister, Holly, then Mom, who showed more steel than fear. We made eye contact, and I tried not to choke up as we exchanged nods. It all happened in a flash, in seconds, then I turned to take my seat and wait quietly with Dan and everyone else for the judge.

The wait gave me time to check out the cameras mounted in the usually empty jury box, most with network logos—the CBS eye, that peacock, the Fox searchlights, and ABC—I knew them all from my favorite kids' shows and Saturday-morning cartoons. How far were those dreamy days from the nightmare of having all those news cameras today pointed at me?

"All rise!" Judge Critchley was back on the bench. Court was officially in session.

And since I was the only item on the morning's agenda, we got right to business. As Dan introduced me, I bowed my head and slouched as low as possible in my chair, wishing I didn't feel so freakishly conspicuous. But there was no hiding. The only obstacle between me and the cameras was a white plastic water jug on the defense table.

Then, with Dan speaking to me but for everyone in the room to hear, I was invited to tell the court—"in your own words"—what exactly made me guilty of passion provocation manslaughter. This was *not* going to be about lessons learned or positive messages to share. All of that would wait for my still-unscheduled sentencing hearing. This allocution was my confession to a lesser charge than murder.

Dan placed a five-page typed statement on the table for me

to read. He would have to turn the pages for me since I couldn't use my cuffed hands, which were shackled to a chain around my waist. I hunched over the defense table to begin reading—then struggled to find my voice.

I sat back. I sat forward. I closed my eyes. I bowed my head. I looked to the ceiling. I looked at my hands. I clenched my jaw. I sucked in air. I exhaled. And with most others in the room holding their breath, I took nearly thirty long, silent seconds to begin—only to freeze and have to start over.

Once I finally found my vocal cords, I was able to begin and keep going, for the first time telling my story to the world:

"From the time I was eight years old until I was twelve years old, I was sexually assaulted and raped by Dennis Pegg. It started with him wanting to touch my scar that I had from open-heart surgery at the age of six. It progressed to wrestling matches and eventually led to him raping me."

The telling did not get any easier as I went on. After describing Pegg's claims of getting drunk and naked with "my close family relation" and with our childhood friend Jeff, all I could think about was my brother, Jay, sitting right behind me as I revealed his secrets, too. I wanted to slide under the defense table. My whole body started shaking from a nervous, bouncing foot. I had to stop and breathe. Dan put a hand on my shoulder, but I could do nothing until my tension eased. I tried rocking back and forth in my seat until I recovered enough to tell the story of Jeff's suicide with a shotgun in 1983, summing it up with:

"I will always believe that Jeff killed himself as a result of Dennis Pegg's abuse."

Talking about Jeff had me in tears. My nose was running. But I had no tissues, and I couldn't raise my shackled hands above the defense table. I kept trying to lean my face close to the tabletop where my fingers could reach to wipe my eyes and nose. I was a mess.

Sharing my childhood terror over Pegg's brutality to animals—and his warnings that he would do the same to me if I told anyone our secrets—left my voice and body shaking again. Every couple of minutes I found myself out of breath, my mouth dry, my body quaking uncontrollably as if with chills and fever. I told the courtroom that fear was one reason why, when my father asked whether Pegg ever hurt me, I always denied it. And another reason:

"For all those years after Dennis Pegg raped me, he was still untouchable because of who he was and what he represented. He was a respected law enforcement officer. He was an expert with guns. He was a Boy Scout leader. No one would ever have believed my word over his."

Dan made certain that my statement noted all the triggering moments and events leading up to the night of June 12, 2012. I described seeing Pegg months earlier at the QuickChek with a boy that I immediately suspected Pegg was molesting. I told the courtroom how affected I had been seeing Jerry Sandusky and that smirk, and about encountering Joe Rubino, the guy who ripped me off in a motorcycle deal, and then telling my friend Bob Reynolds that, no, Rubino was not first on my "hit list"—number one was "the scumbag that raped me when I was a kid."

And, finally, I demonstrated elements of passion provocation, pointing out, "From the time I told Bob that Dennis Pegg had raped me, to the time we went to Pegg's house, was less than half an hour."

The courtroom was silent. Some in the crowd, and even among courthouse staff, wiped their eyes.

After brief discussions between Judge Critchley and the lawyers, the hearing was over. Two guards stepped to my side, ready to take my elbows and escort me out the door and back to the holding area. I stood and looked back at my mom. I think we were both relieved that it was over. I gave her another little nod.

Suddenly, the whole spectator gallery erupted in applause. Most in the audience jumped to their feet—and the judge let it go, never banging his gavel or calling for order in the court. But the unexpected outburst startled the guards, who reflexively shoved me quickly through the open security door and into the holding area. They considered the demonstration a possible security challenge. I considered it a big hug to my family.

Dan came back minutes later to see me in the steel-mesh cage, still shaking his head about the applause. He told me I did well. He also brought along the prosecutor, who he said had asked to speak with me.

Mueller surprised me with an apology: "I'm sorry that the system didn't get Dennis Pegg a long time ago." He assured me that times and investigative protocols had changed and that it was at least less likely today that another kid in Sussex County would go through what I did.

And with that Mueller was off to meet with a couple of Pegg's relatives who had also been in the audience. The prosecutor wanted to assure them that spectators were not applauding

Pegg's death. "That applause was for you," Mueller had told me. "And for what it took for you to finally tell your story."

Again I was left in the custody of my courthouse guards, who moved me from the cage and back to the holding cell.

"Well, wasn't that a fuckin' first?" one of them marveled.

"What d'ya mean?" I asked.

"I've just never seen anyone admit to killing someone and get a standing ovation. Hey, awesome speech, by the way."

Part VI

THE CONVICT

My guilty plea to second-degree manslaughter that summer morning in 2015 made me, by definition, a convicted felon. It also put my immediate future in the hands of one man—Judge Thomas J. Critchley Jr. I didn't know him outside the courtroom, where he always wore a black robe and referred to me as Mr. Fredericks. Imagine, if you can, that some stranger had the authority to send you away to state prison for—go ahead, pick a penalty from five to ten years. It's an awesome and unnerving power to contemplate being aimed at you. He could also rule that I'd already suffered enough. My attorney had filed a motion arguing that the judge should reduce the charges to *third-degree* manslaughter with its reduced sentencing range of three to five years. The math was simple. I'd already served more than three years in the Sussex County jail. So, Judge Critchley also had the power to let me go home. Now.

Chapter Thirty-Six

MATH, MOM,
AND MIRACLES

O n a December morning nearly six months after my court-room confession, I was back in court offering this advice to fellow victims of child abuse and rape: Secrets are toxic. "No matter how painful it may seem," I told another overflow courtroom audience, "I urge everyone to speak out about their traumas and abuse." Sharing that message dressed in my prison stripes and waiting to be sentenced for killing a man, I obviously knew what I was talking about.

And just to be clear, I also told the court and Judge Critch-ley, "I don't recommend that anyone follow in my footsteps." It was part of the more positive message that defense attorney Dan Perez wanted me to project, along with my regrets and remorse, in addressing the judge who was weighing my punishment.

By the winter of 2015 I had completed another round of psych evaluations, this time under the questioning and testing of prosecution expert Louis Schlesinger. His report, like that of

defense expert Dawn Hughes, was filled with clinical terminol-
ogy that summed me up as reasonably well-adjusted, even "quite
friendly . . . pleasant and cooperative." He ruled out "any kind
of underlying psychotic process" and wrote that he found "no
evidence of bizarre or grossly inappropriate behavior or thought
content."

Among his conclusions was what he called "the most out-
standing clinical feature" of his analysis: "the absence of any significant overt psychopathology."

Most important, both forensic psychologists agreed that I did
not have criminal intent, that I was unlikely to "re-offend," and
that I suffered from post-traumatic stress disorder, the result of
abuse and rape over a span of years by Dennis Pegg.

However, Schlesinger's most interesting opinions he saved
for conversations with the prosecution. He told Greg Mueller,
I would later learn, that Clark Fredericks was a decent human
being who would have trouble living with himself unless he paid
some debt to society. Or something like that. Bottom line: for my
own good, I needed some amount of prison time, some measure
of punishment as a form of atonement.

Had I known about it back then, I might have dismissed such
a notion as so much psychobabble, especially as I still hoped that
my three-plus years in the Keogh-Dwyer Correctional Facility
might qualify as sufficient time served, as more than enough
"atonement"—or whatever the psych crowd wanted to call it—to
justify my immediate release.

Meanwhile, Dan continued doing his best to keep my expectations low. No judge likes to go with the lowest end of the sen-

tencing spectrum, he told me—especially on murder cases. And Critchley already had one relatively lenient sentencing decision under appeal in another Mueller prosecution. That one involved a fatal drunk-driving accident. Dan warned that the judge wasn't likely to risk two appeals at the same time for being too soft.

Dan's advice: "You need to prepare for something in the mid-to-high range. Most likely, seven years."

I tried to be prepared. But that morning in December when I made my next penguin walk from the jailhouse to the courthouse, Dan's reality check was no match for my high hopes. And for the next two hours those hopes rose and fell like ocean swells on every observation by the judge.

"I am mindful of the fact that the man who is here being sentenced today did this because of what was done to him," Critchley said.

I silently cheered him on: *Yes! Yes! Yes! That's it.*

But Critchley stopped short of accepting Dan's motion to reduce my charges to third-degree manslaughter and said that nothing justifies vigilante actions.

I tried not to react physically, but inside I groaned.

The judge continued to muse: "I don't feel like I am sentencing someone who was committed to a criminal lifestyle. What happened to him as a child made him snap."

That sounded promising. Again, I was cheered. *Yes! Yes! Yes!*

"It is clear that the young Mr. Fredericks was exploited, abused, and damaged by someone who wormed his way into a position of authority."

Yes! He gets it! Good, good, good!

"And I am tempted to liberate Mr. Fredericks from further custody."

Yes! Please, go for it. Liberate me!

He wouldn't go that far. He said he would sentence me "to the minimum" for second-degree manslaughter—five years. I barely heard the rest, but he added, "I apologize for having to send you to prison for a single day."

Five years was better than my lawyer's prediction. It was also what my mother and I had prayed for.

I told myself I shouldn't be disappointed. The inmate crew up in the 5R tier thought I was the luckiest bro in the building. Even the guards were happy for me. Some offered congratulations.

But one inmate, Posey, didn't see it that way. Not at all. I knew something about his case. I had helped Posey exchange notes with his public defender. During my three years in the jail, the dude had been inside and released only to return a second time after beating up his girlfriend. His pending assault charges carried a hefty fourteen-year sentence—what typically happens, he was certain, when you're arrested while black.

"But you get five years for murder!" he exploded in my face, ranting about white man's privilege, the racist system, the racist jail, the racist courts, the racist country, working himself up for a jailhouse brawl.

"C'mon, bro," I said. "I'm not gonna fight you."

Mostly, I was exhausted from the emotional stress of my sentencing session. Despite the explosion, he was a pal. He came back to apologize fifteen minutes later. Posey wasn't mad at me;

he was mad at the system. As for me, all I wanted to do was read and reflect on what had happened that morning.

I knew one thing: my mom had to be the happiest woman in Sussex County with my sentence now official. We had done the math based on various possibilities, and a ten-year sentence would've kept me in prison into the 2020s, when my mother would be ninety-two years old and counting. Now, with a five-year term—and allowing for early release after serving 85 percent of my time—I could be home in time to help her blow out eighty-seven candles.

She wanted that. I could almost hear her voice already, coming over that scratchy phone connection in the visitors' room this coming Sunday: *I told you so, Clarkie! I believe in God, I believe in prayer, and I still believe in miracles.*

Chapter Thirty-Seven

PRISON INSURANCE

Unfortunately for my mother, she had more than one wounded, middle-aged son dealing with the emotional baggage of childhood sex abuse. My older brother, Jay, still keeping his trauma secrets locked inside, had taken a sharp turn toward alcohol abuse after my arrest for murdering our molester.

Jay had other demons, too, including financial troubles that threatened the tire-and-auto center where I used to work with him. He was forced to close the shop and declare bankruptcy about nine months into my residency at the county jail. And the dominoes kept falling. He lost his thirty-three-acre farm, his heavy drinking compounded other health problems, and his marriage collapsed. Within the year after I went to jail, Jay moved into my old room at home—another grown son back living with his mom.

By all accounts, Jay wasn't interested in therapy. His drinking got so bad that he ended up in an emergency room after falling, taking a face-plant that left him with a broken eye socket. As he was diabetic, his drinking was especially bad for his general health. He suffered a heart attack and needed a pacemaker.

I was just trying to keep my own head above water, wrestling with my own depression and desperation. My only connection with my brother was through weekly reports on his troubles from Mom and Jay's daughter, Kim. I felt helpless. They thought I should talk to my brother directly, and they encouraged Jay to visit me one Sunday.

It didn't work out well. We were both so uncomfortable that our twenty minutes together seemed like hours. It wasn't the right time or place for a heart-to-heart about our shared traumas. It wasn't even the time or place for sympathetic reassurances. Besides, we were both psychological wrecks. The blind were leading the blind. I told my family it wasn't worth pressuring him to come back. He never did.

I blamed Jay's unrelenting downward spiral on Pegg, but I felt guilty, too. In killing our abuser, I had also resurrected all the ghosts my brother had managed to bury for forty years. I had dragged my whole family into the long-running Dennis Pegg scandals of Sussex County. Maybe the worst of it came with my allocution, when I testified that Pegg abused me and a "close family member." Jay had to deal with everyone in our world knowing the secret that he was still trying to hide—even from himself.

Ultimately it was Pegg's fault. When the molester touched me and Jay and our neighbor Jeff, the collateral damage spread through the years to just about everyone who loved us. Now, with Jay's emotional collapse, I couldn't help hating Pegg more every day since I killed him.

It was easy to hate Pegg, even as I was about to celebrate my fourth Christmas in county jail. And *celebrate* was the right word for it. The Keogh-Dwyer Correctional Facility was home now, and I was not looking forward to my anticipated transfer to state prison. The guards went around saying, "Merry Christmas." The jail staff always whipped up special holiday meals. And Christmas Day 2015 fell on a Sunday, visitors' day, so I'd get another chance to celebrate the number 5 with my mother.

When the state prison transport van hadn't arrived by dark on Christmas Eve, I settled in for my long winter's nap. When, all of a sudden, there arose such a clatter—the guards burst in yelling, "Fredericks! Pack up. Now! Let's go. Now!"

I had two minutes to clear out my cell, putting in a garbage bag everything that wasn't promised to other inmates. I had lots of valuables—a couple pillows, blankets, extra socks and under-wear—that I tossed out into the tier for the guys who asked for them. I was allowed to bring along one book. I scooped up my Bible.

Also, I handed over to a trusted inmate friend one large en-velope that I'd already sealed, stamped, and addressed to myself. He would see to it that it went in the jail's outgoing mail the next week. The address included my state prisoner number so the en-velope would find me no matter to which of several state prisons I might be assigned. It contained my clipping file, a collection of newspaper stories about me and my case.

I considered the clippings in that envelope my prison life insurance policy. Experienced inmates had warned me that a white dude of my age with no prior criminal record entering prison for the first time would almost certainly be targeted as a pedophile. I needed to preempt that suspicion before I had my head bashed in, they said.

My press clippings would show that not only was I *not* a pedophile, but that I'd killed one.

Chapter Thirty-Eight

A DIFFERENT VIBE

I would spend Christmas Eve in Trenton, New Jersey, at something called the Central Reception and Assignment Facility—CRAF, for short. Before being sent to one of eight or nine state penitentiaries, I was to be put through medical, dental, and more psychological examinations. Finally, I would be interviewed by a three-member classification board that would determine my assignment.

But I would first be grilled by my bunkmate, an amiable gangbanger with the street name Snap. He was twenty years old and the proud father of four. He missed them on this Christmas Eve. "How many kids you got?" he called up to me on the top bunk from his mattress below. That I had just turned fifty and had no children caught him by surprise. "What? You can't be a man if you don't have kids."

Snap's inner-city neighborhood was such a different world from my rural Sussex County. When I was fishing, he was ducking drive-by shooters. When I was drinking beer and blackberry brandy with a sheriff's officer and Scout leader, he was packing a pistol to grade school for self-defense. He wasn't what I imagined about gang members, either. He was smart and open and laughed easily, a likable kid in any setting.

We were just getting to know each other when all the lights in the cell went out. We'd have to get used to that. The nightly witching hour would always be at ten. A few minutes later, Snap started cursing frantically. In the sudden darkness, he had noticed shadowy movement on the floor. "Mice!" he shouted. "They're everywhere."

I tried to assure him that the rodents were more scared of him, but I was having my own Christmas Eve nightmare—cockroaches on the walls and ceiling. At least with the lights on, I could see them. In the dark, I imagined them falling into the top bunk with me. What a hellhole. Who could have known how much I'd already be missing the Sussex County jail?

Near the end of my six-day stopover at CRAF, I was finally summoned for the classification-board interview. A group of two or three dozen of us were crammed into a single, small holding cell "elbow to asshole," as someone complained, waiting to go before the board one at a time. No one could move, so we made noise. Lots of noise, a mix of complaints and profanity. One guard, a big and burly dyspeptic dude, kept demanding quiet, to not a single decibel of difference. At one point he threatened, convincingly I feared, to turn his chemical Mace on the entire holding cell.

Then, he was called to deliver me to my board interview. I was escorted into a mostly empty gymnasium-type space. The board members sat at a table on an elevated stage, looking down at a floor that may once have been a basketball court. A single chair on that open floor was waiting for me.

My surly guard more or less shoved me down into that chair and remained standing next to me with his arms folded. No one spoke for a few moments as the three people onstage leafed through what I presumed was my record.

Finally, the head guy looked up and said, "Mr. Fredericks, I've been doing this for a long time, and I have to say—I've never seen somebody come through CRAF with a five-year sentence for murder." He seemed puzzled. "I've never seen that. Can you explain to me how you got that sentence?"

I took a deep breath and launched into an abbreviated version, maybe a minute or two of who, what, when, and how I was triggered—before I said, "and then I slit his throat." But for all the times I'd told the story—to forensic psychologists, a lawyer, and a courtroom full of people—it was still raw and emotional to me. I had choked up immediately, tears washing down my face, sniffling through every word. And that big cranky guard reached down and put a big gentle hand on my shoulder and left it there. The guy shouting threats minutes earlier softly encouraged me, "Take your time. Take a breath. No rush."

When I finished, I could see all three board members nodding their heads. "I understand, Mr. Fredericks. Are you open to therapy," the head guy said.

"Yes," I said through my sniffles.

"Well, Northern State [Prison] has the best therapists. I'd like to send you there. If I do that, will you get involved in therapy?"

I assured him I would.

He wished me luck, all three of them smiling.

My guard reached down at the same time to take one arm and helped me up from the chair. He was like a different man. And he wasn't taking me back through the holding cell, either. As we stepped out a side door, I was still wiping my eyes and sniffling.

"Just stay here and chill out. Catch your breath. Compose yourself," he said. "I don't want to take you past the holding cell with tears in your eyes. Those guys are animals."

He had to go back to the holding area, but he walked me to another hallway and said it would lead back to my tier of cells. When I was ready, I could just follow that hall and make a left at the end. No escort required.

"And they're right about Northern State," he said as we parted. "It has the best therapists. I'm sorry about what happened to you."

Another guard, a regular on the night shift, came into my cell the next evening. He was at least as bad-humored as the guy threatening to mace the entire holding cell—big, burly, and mean as a rattlesnake. The night guy was always threatening to take people into the closet, out of camera range, to smash their faces.

So, when the night guy barged into my cell barking, "Fredericks!," I immediately jumped down from my bunk so as not to keep him waiting.

"What is it?" I said.

He handed me a garbage bag and told me to pack up my things and bring it out to his office on the tier. "You're shipping out in the morning."

When I got to his office with my garbage bag, I was fourth and last in line to check in. He attached my name tag to my bag and sat back and said, "Do you mind if I ask you a question?"

Of course not. I just shrugged.

"I just wanna know . . . Dude, what did you do to end up in here? What's your crime?"

The other inmates had all gone. For the private audience, I gave him my one-minute version and got through it without choking up. He listened, leaning back in his chair, both hands clasped behind his head, nodding. He seemed to approve of my crime, finally saying, "That was all right by my book."

I couldn't help noticing that he had not asked the previous inmates anything at all about their crimes. "Why did you ask me?"

"You're different, Fredericks. You've got a totally different vibe from what I see coming through here."

So, I'm different, too? Maybe I had a lot to learn from prison.

Chapter Thirty-Nine

EMOTIONAL MUSCLE

N othing about Northern State Prison said "home sweet home"—it was mostly fortresslike concrete buildings, guard towers, and razor wire. And I wasn't looking forward to a warm welcome. Still, I hoped to adjust quickly and resume my self-improvement efforts—some sort of physical fitness activities and Bible study—like my routine back in the Sussex County jail.

I wasn't sure what to expect of the promise of therapy that got me assigned to such a forbidding piece of real estate. It sure didn't look like a place to heal or grow emotionally. It looked like punishment and soul-sucking defeat. And waiting for me inside was the one constant of prison life: human degradation. It began almost immediately.

The corrections officer processing my arrival and intake paperwork kept me waiting as he looked through my file. He seemed puzzled, as if something was missing.

"What's your gang name?" he growled.

"I don't have a gang."

He seemed annoyed. "Then, what's your street name?"

"I don't have a street name."

He glared at me. "You're trying to tell me you're in here for murder and you don't have a street name? Don't fuck with me, Fredericks—you'll regret it!"

I regretted it already, especially when he persisted. "What's your alias?"

"I don't have an alias." I knew it was the wrong answer even as the words came out of my mouth.

His explosion of profanities came with a spray of saliva that made me flinch.

Still, I tried to respond politely. "Sir, I come from the country, the hills of northern New Jersey. We don't have gangs in Stillwater."

A few more profanities later he checked off some boxes on my paperwork and ordered me to strip naked, then sit on a chair equipped with an X-ray device. It would reveal whether I was concealing any contraband in my anal cavity.

Yes, prison is that kind of place. You have no privacy, no rights, no dignity. Yet, inmates are supposed to heal, grow, and return to society as improved humans. Fortunately for me, I only needed to survive about nine months here before reaching my release eligibility date. On day one, I was already counting those days.

Once I was cleared by negative X-ray results, my scowling admitting officer tossed me a pillow and blankets and said I was assigned to Unit C—"down that hallway and through the double doors—they'll tell ya your cell."

This time I wasn't shackled and shuffling penguin-style down that long hall. But I was also unescorted and unfamiliar with how to open the locked double doors. I pushed. They didn't move. I waved. They didn't respond to motion. I touched a button on the wall. Nothing happened. After another minute or more pushing, knocking, and looking for some hidden sensor to activate, I heard a familiar angry voice screaming over the hall loudspeaker:

"What the fuck's wrong? Can't you open a fuckin' door?"

"Obviously not, sir." I was unsure he could even hear me. He told me emphatically that I should hit the button on the wall, the same one I had pressed earlier. This time I smacked it with my fist.

Ta-da! I was on my way. A couple other doors later I was admitted to Unit C. It was *not* the fiftieth floor of the Taj Mahal. Hell, it wasn't even the Keogh-Dwyer Correctional Facility. My cell was tiny compared to the one in Sussex County. Imagine a small walk-in closet with two guys living in it, and not even a small window to the outside world.

My cellmate, already well into a decade-long sentence, had filled a pair of personal storage bins that were taking up more of the limited floor space. Adding to the general claustrophobic effect was my bunkie's laundry—white underwear mostly—hanging from a makeshift clothesline strung from a bunk-bed post to a small desk.

There wasn't room enough—between beds and toilet and bins—to stretch out and do a single push-up. My arrival clearly wasn't welcomed by the dude with his laundry drying. I was still standing among his damp shorts and T-shirts, wondering whether to make my bed or just flop down on it, when the guy greeted me with a question:

"You Muslim or Christian?"

"I'm a Christian."

"Good. So am I. But if you touch any of my shit, I'll kill ya."

There was no twinkle in his eyes. It was a rule, not a joke. I gave him a nod and flopped down on my bare mattress. It was the middle of the day; no rush to make my bed. Besides, I still wanted to savor the moment: at least no one was yelling curses at me.

A couple hours later there was a knock at our cell door. I heard a woman's voice calling, "Mr. Fredericks? Mr. Fredericks?" A woman of about sixty was standing just outside the window of our cell door. She was not wearing the uniform of a corrections officer.

I was about to meet Ms. Burger, the prison's clinical social worker. Her voice was coming through the small gap where the cell door latched and locked electronically to the doorjamb. The gap allowed us to speak at a conversational level while leaning close to that crack between door and wall. The awkward arrangement meant no need to shout, but no eye contact through the window, either.

"I can't believe you're here," she said. "I've followed your case on the news. I run counseling sessions, and I wonder if you would be willing to join me for one-on-one therapy?"

Of course! She was the reason they'd sent me to the Newark prison. Maybe I would come to appreciate this place after all. It was, at least, reassuring. I slept well that first night. No mice.

No cockroaches. And my bunkie offered to let me listen to music on his Walkman.

My first meeting face-to-face with Ms. Burger was for an hour in an empty classroom. We talked about my childhood, Dennis Pegg, and my trauma. She talked to me about PTSD. For the first time since I was told that I suffered from traumatic stress, I was offered advice on how to cope, and eventually to beat it. I needed to work on my emotional muscle, she said, as much as my physical strength.

To that end, she asked me to consider joining a new session she was organizing—group therapy for inmates with childhood trauma issues. It turned out that Northern State had so many that she had to limit the size of her group. Our weekly group ranged in size from six to twelve. The stories I heard ranged from horrific to unimaginable. The abuse was physical, emotional, sexual. One kid was burned all over his body by red-hot hangers heated over the stove. Another had his head held underwater in the bathtub. Another was banished for days at a time to a pitch-black basement without food, heat, or a toilet. I thought their treatment was the worst. They thought mine was the worst.

It turned out to be incredibly therapeutic.

Before I'd found Ms. Burger, my only conversations about my abuse and trauma had been under duress—forced to tell state- and defense-selected psychologists, my lawyer, and a courtroom full of cameras and a judge the story that might save me years in prison. None of that was therapeutic. But sharing with Ms. Burger was voluntary. Our group was voluntary. We got vulnerable together. And, yes, that *was* incredibly therapeutic.

It was not, however, easy.

Ms. Burger did not tiptoe around anyone's weaknesses. She was there to help, not coddle. In one blunt assessment, she told me, "You really haven't shown much self-discipline at any time in your life, have you?"

It was a reference to my history of addictions. I guess she had been counting all the ways I'd hidden from or disguised my fears—the compulsive gambling, serial sex and one-nighters, alcohol abuse, pill popping, and drug fogs.

She suggested that I focus on self-discipline right then and there, in prison, of all places. It came down to a simple reality check: "You will need that discipline next year on the outside."

What if I can finally control the addictions that have come to control me? Is it possible to develop enough emotional muscle to never again experience such a powerful triggering provocation?

Chapter Forty

GOD HELP ME

O nly a few weeks after my arrival a guy on my tier over-dosed on heroin, revealing one of the surprising truths of prison life—even a tough place like Northern State had a drug problem. Heroin was everywhere. A couple of inmates OD'd and died during my stretch. The dealers or their spotters spotted me early.

I always had a lot of commissary spending money, thanks to my mother, Niece Kim, and a lot of friends keeping my prison account full. I'd come back from a shopping run with a couple garbage bags of pens and paper, snacks, and other things. Inmates noticed that kind of consumption. "Hey, man—you want some heroin?" "Hey, man—you prefer cocaine? I got a buddy at the hospital can get whatever you want." It was constant. Someone was always hounding me.

Marijuana was in plentiful supply, too. Its telltale aroma made it a delicacy for use only in proximity to a cell toilet. The prison commodes, much like airplane toilets, functioned with a powerful suction that swept away everything, including smoke. You could tell if your bunkie was smoking dope because he had to keep flushing repeatedly with his face in the john.

And then there was prison hooch. One guy a couple cells down on my tier had the local concession and his very own moonshine recipe, using our prison meals. The key ingredients: stale bread, aged fruit, and lots of sugar tossed together in a plastic garbage bag, allowed to ferment under the bunks for a week or so, then strained and stored in empty water bottles. Best served mixed with fresh orange juice.

Guys buying it were getting absolutely pumped. I mean, fall-down drunk. I had a standing invitation to partake to my heart's content. The local winemaker knew my story and why I was doing time and said he approved. "Hey, man, for what you did, you take as many bottles as you want anytime." I thanked him for his generosity but demurred. "I'm good, bro."

That first OD on my tier introduced me to some other truths about life in Northern State Prison. For example, one inmate's overdose was bad news for everyone on the tier. Not because anyone cared about the guy one way or another, but because of the COs' crackdown that would inevitably follow. In that first case, our entire tier population was marched down to the gymnasium and lined up to provide urine tests.

That, in turn, brought the hammer down on another half dozen guys who tested positive for . . . something. Meanwhile, up on the tier, other corrections officers with their drug-sniffing dog were busy trashing our cells. They called it a search for contraband. So, why then, I wanted to ask, did they squeeze out all the contents of a ketchup container onto the cell floor?

You get the picture of a typical day, a reasonably good day, in the life of us inmates. Insults piled upon indignities and served up with brutish indifference. This was where I had to find ways to master self-discipline, to prepare myself for life back in polite society.

My first challenge was to keep busy. I signed up for rec (recreation) to continue my physical workout routines. I signed up for Northern State's version of Bible study. I started attending the prison church services on Sunday—the most spirited spiritual service this Episcopalian had ever joined—with gospel music, dancing, and a great deal of joyful-noise making. I still had both one-on-one therapy with Ms. Burger as well as her weekly group sessions. I started taking meditation training. (I also started making notes and writing the remembrances that would form the basis of this book.)

But what about something more demanding than putting pressure on my time and attention? What about something that changed old habits, or something that tested my will?

Church and Bible study had reminded me just how often I blurted out *God damn*s and *Jesus fucking Christ*s. I made a vow to God and myself to better control my language and to stop breaking the third commandment. I would never again take the Lord's name in vain.

Another test would come out of my natural and sometimes powerful sexual urges. Again, I vowed to God and myself that I was going to resist those natural forces and stop masturbating.

The new Clark, the now-determined and self-disciplined version of that former addict and triggered-stress victim, was going to declare his emotional independence with a display of resolve and willpower—a weeklong fast. Inspired by the Ramadan fasting by my Muslim prison mates, I vowed to God and myself and Ms. Burger that I would consume no food from dawn to sunset for seven days.

"God, help me, give me strength," I prayed.

Fasting was the greatest and most concentrated challenge. Nagging hunger messed with my meditation, my reading and writing, even my praying. I had to moderate my daily workout schedule in the face of a protein deficiency as the week went on. Through it all, I learned something critical about myself. If I could say no to food—not just drugs or pills or any other pleasures, but one of the necessities of life—then I was stronger than I had ever imagined. It was an exhilarating discovery.

It did not, however, change my quality of life. I still woke up every morning in the same hellhole. My newest bunkie was a twenty-year-old Bloods gang kid who took one look at this middle-aged white cellmate and declared, "If you're a fuckin' kiddie toucher, I'm gonna fuck you up." So, for the first time since checking in to Northern State, I had to pull out my prison insurance papers, my clip files. Seeing what I did to another "kiddie toucher" seemed to ease his mind. "Ah, that's cool," he said.

Still, he turned out to be the bunkie from hell, starting with his officially being a Code Red—a suicide risk. Because of that, he was a walking, talking—especially talking—consumer of prison-approved antipsychotic medications. He offered to share.

"I'm good, bro," I told him. "I'm putting my drug days behind me."

Over the weeks and months that followed, the ready availability of prison dope and hooch offered repeated opportunities for me to reconsider my abstinence. But I also noticed that saying "No, thanks" seemed to be getting easier and easier.

Chapter Forty-One

NO PLACE LIKE HOMELESS

B y early summer 2016 I was into my last hundred days of
incarceration—at least by my calculations. Based on a five-
year prison sentence, less nearly thirteen hundred days already
served in the Sussex County jail, and allowing for parole after
serving a total of 85 percent of those five years behind bars, I put
my earliest release date on a Tuesday in mid-September, give or
take a couple of leap-year adjustments.

The New Jersey State Parole Board maintained an office in
the prison to help prepare and process inmates due for release
on probation. I was summoned to that office in August, expecting to learn my official date for "graduation," or whatever they
called it. What the prison parole officer called it was a snafu.
He said the Sussex County prosecutor's office had failed to up-
date my record to reflect my manslaughter guilty plea. As a result, he said, "Your paperwork still has you down as a convicted
murderer."

Everyone knew that record was outdated, but until it was officially corrected, I had to get used to waiting a little longer. "You're
not getting out in September," the man said. Let the record get
straightened out, he assured me, and my parole would be treated
as routine and subject to the usual and ordinary restrictions for
a second-degree manslaughter violation. Otherwise, he warned,
I risked standing before a parole board made up mostly of law
enforcement and correctional officers contemplating the severity of parole restrictions for someone who murdered not only a
fellow law enforcement officer but one who had also supervised
a county jail.

I couldn't argue with the logic of his caution or the unfortu-
nate timing of it all. Besides, things weren't good at home, either. Friends and family advised me that when I was released, I'd
have to stay away from my hard-drinking brother. They worried
that Jay might be a bad influence on me, that his drinking might
tempt me back into alcohol abuse. My lawyer strongly recommended that I not move back into my mom's house. Even my
own mother was making me feel unwelcomed. Jay had moved
into my old room, and she didn't have the heart to kick him out
of the house.

"I don't want Jay living in his truck and drinking himself to
death," she said.

I couldn't blame her for it. That was my mom. Her moth-
erly love endured just about everything. I, for one, should have
known that a long time ago, dating back to my own dark days
of drug and alcohol fogs. That was the same woman who was
ready to run off to the ends of the earth with me after I murdered

someone. I couldn't very well second-guess her care and com-passion for my wounded brother.

That's when I turned to Ms. Burger during one of our therapy sessions for a different kind of advice. I told her I might need help finding housing on the outside, when the time for my re-lease came. There was no rush though. Even after Greg Mueller got my prison paperwork updated, the parole people kept bounc-ing me from one release date to another. First, it was February. Then it was late January.

The dead of winter seemed a particularly tough time of year for a prisoner to be hitting the streets without a home. Ms. Burger preemptively found me a half dozen homeless shelters that could help keep me off the streets—and that could offer my parole officer a residential address, required as a condition for release on probation.

In December my release date was moved up again, this time to early January. My days of incarceration were coming to a close. I wrote to a friend in Stillwater, asking to room with him, but he couldn't help; he had a new girlfriend who had just moved in.

I reviewed Ms. Burger's list of homeless shelters with dismay. While they were likely to be dry and warm—and would satisfy the parole board requirement that I have an address where I could be found—the shelters were all some distance away from my friends and family. I called home to press the issue. I really didn't want to move into some homeless shelter full of strangers. At least in prison I had friends. I wanted to go *home*. I assured my family there was no need to worry about my falling off the wagon. I wasn't the Clark Fredericks that woke up in that suicide cell so many years ago. I didn't even need my old bedroom. "I'll sleep on the couch," I begged my mother.

Then they moved up my release date yet again—to the next Friday! I had to arrange transit to wherever I was going—someone could pick me up or the state would provide bus fare—and I had to do it soon. I had to pick an address.

"Please, Mom," I pleaded with her, "just let me get the hell out of here. I don't have time to plan somewhere else to go."

She relented. Niece Kim would be waiting for me just outside the prison gates on the morning of December 30, 2016. My mom's hesitation about having me move back in was no reflection of her feelings toward me. To prove the point, she promised to bake my favorite dinner—her special lasagna.

I just wasn't sure I could trust the prison system to let me out when it promised. But to my relief, on the morning of December 30—

"Fredericks! Step out! You're released," barked a guard over the loudspeaker at 7:00 a.m. sharp. My door immediately unlocked with a loud clang. Inmates up and down our tier gathered at their doors to call out best wishes as I passed. Most offered some version of "Good luck." I heard one voice bellow, "And don't come back!"

That was my favorite.

As promised, Kim was waiting for me in her car just outside the last locked gate. When it opened to let me walk out of Northern State Prison, I was free.

Sort of. I was still subject to three years of parole supervision—starting immediately. Among the rules were no drinking, no dope, no out-of-state travel without permission, no over-night stays outside of my authorized residence without prior approval—things like that. As if to emphasize that point, even before heading home to Stillwater, I had to have Kim drive me to Passaic to meet and check in with Melissa Cantinieri, my parole officer.

It was an inauspicious beginning. Ms. Cantinieri wasn't expecting me. Her exact words of greeting were "What the hell are you doing here?"

In all the confusion about my changing release dates, I guess no one had notified my official monitors. That she seemed to blame *me* for showing up unannounced was not a promising sign for what I hoped would be a smooth, no-drama three years.

At last Kim and I reached Stillwater around three o'clock in the afternoon. My eighty-seven-year-old mom was waiting at the same door I had stepped through to surrender to the police 1,661 days before. I reached out to wrap her slight frame in my arms and hold her.

Part VII

NOW WHAT?

When I walked out of prison on the eve of 2017, I had left behind most of the demons I came in with. The triggered addict arrested for murder in his mid-forties was leaving older, the *fifty-one-year-old me*, but also drug-free, alcohol-free, and anger-free—finally rid of the ghosts that had haunted me since childhood. Could it be that this soul-sucking prison had been a blessing in the end? I would sure put Ms. Burger in the blessings category, along with experiences I shared with my group therapy brothers. Taking on the challenge of self-discipline had also been a life changer, adding layer upon layer of emotional muscle where I needed it most. That's why deep in my heart I already knew the truth: prison saved my life. The one question that only time and I could answer was what to do now with this new Clark Fredericks.

Chapter Forty-Two

A SEARCH FOR MEANING

L ife in county jail had been like a spa compared to Northern State Prison. Hardly a day had gone by there without some prison guard threatening grave harm—typically at full volume and salted with f-bombs. It might be some variation of "Everybody down! Kiss that floor or you die on it." Or my personal favorite: "Touch that Bible and I'll break every bone in your hand." It didn't matter what the context was. Mostly, it was guards being guards. Inmates adjusted by being subservient or waiting for permission to do much of anything, to avoid setting off some spit-spewing corrections officer.

My prison-instilled timidity was very much on display in those first few hours out of confinement. Before heading home in my après-prison outfit of slippers, sweatpants, and a sweatshirt, Kim took me to a Kohl's department store for a new wardrobe. While shopping, I hesitated to go alone and find a public restroom. I didn't want to risk getting lost, going down the wrong hallway, picking the wrong door. I asked her to show me the way.

"Really?" she said, surprised that her simple directions weren't enough. Yes, her institutionalized uncle was going to need help and patience easing back into civilized society.

For the next few months, that meant no big homecoming parties. More than anything else, I wanted peace and quiet while reacquainting myself with the gentle rhythms of Stillwater. I took long walks alone. I visited old friends one at a time. I slept past 7:00 a.m. And eventually, I relaxed knowing no one was going to menace my life or bark at me for moving too fast or too slow or too anything else.

I had one of my first reunions with a former customer at Jay's tire-and-auto shop who had sent me dozens of books during my years in custody. Michelle treated me to lunch at a diner. She also gave me a few hundred dollars to help me get back on my feet financially. Other friends and former biker buddies slipped me cash for a new car. I picked out a fifteen-year-old Chevy Monte Carlo for $2,700. It represented freedom, as well as mobility.

Finding work was challenging. I applied for jobs, all sorts of jobs. But my résumé had this five-year gap from 2012 to 2017 with no employment and no explanation. So, although I had graduated with honors from Northeastern University, no one called back. It made me wonder, What sort of future might await my old bunkie Snap, who didn't even have the benefit of a high school diploma or a few references outside those in the gang world?

One of my first steps, as a free man, was to rejoin the gym where I used to work out. My exercise in recent years had been limited to push-ups—and more push-ups. Robin, the owner, welcomed me home with a free six-month membership, including personal training. I was back, this time without steroids. And it felt great.

I started going to church on Sundays with my mother at the same Episcopal church where her minister had told us to pray for the number 5. He invited me back to his office for a private conversation. I gave him a playful swat on the shoulder and joked, "Why didn't you tell us to pray for the number three?"

On Wednesday evenings I attended the evangelical church of Brother Bob, my jailhouse Bible study teacher. He took me aside to say that his church was planning a big group baptism service, total immersions, using steel tubs built by New Jersey prison inmates. I agreed to be among those to be baptized. It also gave me my first public appearance—before a congregation of about five hundred—to share my story of darkness and toxic secrets and recovery and answered prayers.

The crowd response, an emotional outpouring of support and goodwill, was heartwarming. It also reinforced a growing conviction I had that maybe I could help other victims of child abuse by sharing what I had learned, by trying to use my story to inform and inspire and motivate others to speak out. It felt like an exciting prospect.

I knew I was something of a curiosity in the community of former child abuse victims. The mail I'd received through three years in jail, coming from all parts of the country, was phenomenal—thousands of cards and letters. Guards joked that the Keogh-Dwyer Correctional Facility was sometimes like the North Pole Post Office at Christmastime. "No one gets mail like you. I've never seen this before," one guard told me. Televised coverage of my allocution and sentencing hearings would later draw nearly a million views on YouTube.

It made me think, *What if telling my story can save other kids from the hell I went through? What if I can do something important and helpful on behalf of other abuse victims and turn my suffering into meaningful work? How's that, Victor Frankl— how's that for finding meaning in my life?*

A woman in the church audience at my baptism and public testimony invited me to talk to a college criminal justice class. That appearance led to more speaking invitations and, soon afterward, to my introduction into politics. I was invited to join an advocacy group working to change New Jersey's statute of limitations law. The old law, which protected predators, required victims to come forward within two years of reaching adulthood—by legal definition, their eighteenth birthday. Otherwise, they forfeited any right to sue their abusers or the organizations employing those abusers.

The new law under debate at the statehouse in Trenton would allow childhood victims to come forward into their middle age, up to fifty-five years old—a recognition that the average child sex abuse victim is unlikely to confide that experience with anyone else until he or she is an adult—on average, at least forty-two years old. Both the Catholic Church and the Boy Scouts, widely accused of having pedophiles in their ranks, lobbied against such reforms.

I knew almost nothing about such legal issues back before I became an adult. There had been little or no discussion surrounding such statutes of limitations back then. Even as an adult, and as something of a poster boy for just how bad things could get for victims of predators, such debate didn't cross my radar. Only when I considered joining legal actions against the Boy Scouts, months after my prison release, was I told, "Sorry, you can't sue in New Jersey," and the reality of the circumstances struck me.

It was on the statehouse steps in Trenton that I made my public debut as an advocate for reform of New Jersey's outdated child sex abuse statute of limitations law. Community organizers had brought in a busload of supporters from around the state. There were flags and placards, such as the ones proclaiming SEXUAL ABUSE OF LITTLE BOYS AND GIRLS IS SOUL MURDER and END THE STATUTE OF LIMITATIONS ON SEX ABUSE. Reporters took notes on that cold and blustery day as victim after victim shared personal accounts of their frustrations and failures when seeking justice.

After fifteen years of persistent but unsuccessful advocacy by several support groups, there was finally reason to be hopeful. Both houses of the state legislature were considering language on a bill that would make New Jersey one of the most aggressive states in the country removing long-held limits on child sex abuse litigation.

I was the last speaker to step up to the microphone, the cleanup hitter, the grand finale. I brought along with me a five-foot length of rope. I talked about learning how to tie knots. Tying various knots was an essential test for any child who wanted to graduate from the Cub Scouts and become a Boy Scout.

What I learned from the Scouts instead was betrayal. I had lost my innocence when I was raped by my scoutmaster.

For me and every kid like me, the state's statute of limitations was "unacceptable." It left us no meaningful recourse. By the time I was an adult, I already knew too many friends and neighbors who had been damaged by their childhood trauma, driven to suicide or lost to addictions. Just talking about it in this setting, with this crowd of victims and their families, was making me angry again. Not angry for me, but for all those victims still lost, still hurting, still suffering and confused and thinking they had no way out.

"Let's pray that our legislators hear us loud and clear," I said to the crowd, leaning closer to the microphone and addressing those inside the statehouse. "If you don't change this law," I warned, my voice rising in outrage, "there will be blood on your hands!"

Chapter Forty-Three

THE COP AND ME

It took months but I finally found a job, no résumé required, as an assistant chef at the Boat House bar and restaurant on Swartswood Lake. Kathy, owner of the popular dinner spot, knew me and my family. She extended the offer through my brother, Jay, when he stopped in for lunch and she asked about me.

Employment made me happy. It may have made Ms. Cantinieri, my parole officer, even happier. It offered a nice place for food and drinks—and for tracking down her parolee for surprise urine tests.

Owner Kathy was also accommodating as my schedule grew with more speaking engagements and increasingly demanding advocacy work in the state capital. But parole restrictions were a constant reminder that my freedom was tenuous. I was expected to be at home or at work or commuting in between unless I notified Ms. Cantinieri. Not even as a child had my mother had such close oversight of me.

One night driving home from the Boat House after eleven I was pulled over by a state trooper for speeding on the empty highway, but no doubt also for suspicion of drinking and driving. Five years earlier, that would have been a valid suspicion. But not that night. I hadn't taken even a sip of alcohol since my arrest. No ticket was issued, but the trooper ran my license number through the state database. And that's how Ms. Cantinieri learned of my otherwise uneventful contact with law enforcement. Technically, I should have let her know immediately.

She called early and hostile the next morning. "You didn't call me!"

"It was eleven oh four p.m.," I tried to explain.

"Don't let it happen again."

I knew full well that threats to my continuing freedom were very real. A former inmate buddy of mine answered his front door after work one night to find his parole officer outside. Unfortunately for my buddy, when he opened that door, he was holding a can of beer. He was back in prison that same night, finishing his remaining eighteen months in custody.

One day I arrived in the early afternoon for my kitchen shift at the Boat House and was just getting into my chef's gear when Shannon, our bartender, came back looking nervous and reluctant. I waited.

"Clark, there are a couple guys at the bar. I thought they were fishermen. They want me to tell you . . ." She stopped. "They said you wouldn't mind, but . . ."

"I wouldn't mind what? Who are they?" I figured some jokester friends might be pulling some sort of practical joke.

Shannon finally just blurted it out: "These guys are from the state police. They want to see you."

I laughed. If this was official police business, they wouldn't have sent the bartender. Besides, I'd done nothing since June of 2012 to deserve arrest. I tossed my apron aside and headed out to the bar. I'd seen those guys sitting out there when I came in, but they weren't in uniform, and they had their backs to me. All I knew about them was that they'd ordered burgers and beers.

When they turned to face me, the one I recognized was grinning like he knew all my secrets. He pretty much did—though we'd met only once a long time ago, on June 13, 2012. He was my arresting officer.

This was the state investigator who booked me for murder, the forensics guy who knew I was one of Pegg's victims from the clues he saw at the crime scene, the cop who, as I sat there oozing blood and chained to a wall, apologized for law enforcement's failure to investigate Pegg, the dude that looked me in the eye and insisted I talk to no one else in the state police building unless and until I had a lawyer present, and who then privately arranged for that first lawyer to intervene on my behalf.

Yeah, that guy. It was Officer Howard Ryan of the New Jersey State Police.

Right there, at the Boat House bar, I threw both arms around him and gave him the bear hug I'd owed him for five years.

Me and Howie would end up the best of friends, even making appearances together at some of my speaking engagements, making us an odd couple to some: the cop and the cop killer. We still talk and laugh and dine together. When Howie was diagnosed with colon cancer a few years ago, I was one of the first people he called to share the news.

He also asked for a favor. "I want you to pray for me."

"Really? Why me?"

He just smiled. "After what you went through and what you did—and only got five years—well, I'm thinking if anyone's got a connection with the Man Upstairs, you're the one."

Chapter Forty-Four

MY AUDIENCE

Sometime after coming home from prison, while working out at the gym, I ran into Sussex County sheriff Mike Strada. We were both sweating at the weight machines. It was a cordial encounter. The sheriff welcomed me back to town and said that I should call him if I ever needed his assistance. Only in a small town, right? The county's top sheriff exchanging pleasantries with the local boy who had murdered a retired sheriff's lieutenant. Of course, Sheriff Strada knew my case and all its complexities.

But his offer intrigued me. I kicked it around for several months before settling on a plan. "I'd like a chance to speak to the inmates," I finally told Strada.

It had occurred to me while looking for places to share my story—hoping to use my experiences as inspiration or motivation for anyone else struggling with addictions, childhood abuse, and other traumas—that the jail where I hit rock bottom was a natural place to talk about it. Brother Bob, my jailhouse Bible study pastor, offered to let me use one of his weekly time slots. I picked the Monday after Thanksgiving 2018.

What a difference six years, five months, and thirteen days makes—from the time in 2012 when I arrived as a suspect under arrest. This time my official greeting committee included the sheriff's secretary, Hilary Manser, and Undersheriff John Tomasula. There were no shackles. No handcuffs. No getting chained to the wall. Nothing but handshakes and hugs from all the guards.

I waited at the elevator to shake the hand of each inmate as he arrived on the second floor. One of the faces was familiar—a former bunkie who was back doing time. I introduced myself to the group as a former resident of tier 5R-T for three and a half years. I told them I had killed the pedophile cop who raped me when I was twelve.

While telling them about my first morning in jail, about waking up in the suicide cell facing a life sentence, I described my panic sensations: "I felt like I was drowning, like I was gasping for breath." I could see several heads nodding as if they'd been there, done that, too. I suggested we all take a look at Psalms 69:

Save me, O God, for the waters have come up to my neck . . .
the floods engulf me.
I am worn-out calling for help; my throat is parched.

My eyes fail, looking for my God. . . .
Many are my enemies . . . who seek to destroy me.

I talked about having reached a critical point in my life while sitting upstairs in my cell. I realized I had to change *me*, that I had to soften my heart and develop faith if I ever hoped to find some inner peace. Up to that point, to the extent that I could tolerate religion at all, I had treated God like a lucky rabbit's foot and prayer as a hedge against risky behavior, figuring a little extra protection couldn't hurt. But I never read the Bible. Not ever. Not until I signed up for Brother Bob's Bible study class to get some time away from my cell.

What had surprised me, back then, was finding encouragement in a book written thousands of years ago that described so much of what I was going through, especially the challenge of overcoming my addictions. I also read them an excerpt from New Testament book of Romans, chapter 7:

I do not understand what I do, for what I want to do, I do not do,
but what I hate, this I keep doing.

How many of us could have written that? I wondered aloud. On the other hand, the same Bible makes a case for coming to terms with hardships and setbacks as learning experiences, as tests that make us stronger. For that, our Bible study session moved on to consider the New Testament book of James:

Consider it pure joy when you face trials of many kinds,
because the testing of your faith produces perseverance,
and perseverance must finish its work,
so, you are mature and complete.

It was my goal now to show them through my example that there could be life after incarceration—life that wasn't defined by mistakes and failures—something I would myself be working on for the rest of my days. I told them how I was directing my energies to help a team of advocates in Trenton reform the statute of limitations law, my way of turning the worst moments of my life into something positive, my way of helping other victims. I had good news to share about that, too.

By the end of 2018, that reform legislation, known as the Child Victims Act, was finally moving toward a vote. And while the new law couldn't prevent pedophile predators from doing harm, it could at least make it possible for victims to go after financial sanctions. That alone could be a lifesaver for trauma sufferers who, unlike me, might not have the support of family and friends and a great lawyer.

I wound up my pep talk to the Bible study group at Keogh-Dwyer Correctional Facility by going back thirty-five hundred years to the book of Genesis. It was another verse that could have been written for me. As I apply it to my life, it suggests that all the suffering and torment inflicted on me by Dennis Pegg, and my guilt and punishment for killing him, had brought me to an unlikely place—preparing me to be an instrument to help and encourage others.

You intended to harm me, God intended it for good,
to accomplish what is now being done . . .
the saving of many lives.

The mood on the visitors' floor was almost festive as the inmates headed back to the elevators and their cells. Instead of the more formal handshakes they offered as we first greeted each other, this time every one of them gave me a hug and a pat on the back.

You can imagine my sense of accomplishment—bringing encouragement and maybe some measure of hope to guys who, like me, dealt with feelings of hopelessness every morning they woke up in a jail cell.

I made similar connections with other audiences. Fresh out of prison I had asked myself, *What if I can help dudes like me find the will and a way to get up off the floor, off drugs and alcohol, and out of the downward spiral that nearly destroyed me?* That question prompted me to focus on substance abuse centers scattered across northern New Jersey for my first speaking tour. At these centers, addicts were going through torments and frustrations that I knew only too well.

From day one, my pitch followed a pattern:

"Okay, I want you all to be honest with me," I said to start every session. "How many of you in this room feel defeated?" Typically, most people's hands went up. Then I asked, "How many of you feel you can still achieve the goals and dreams that you had for your life before you wound up here, in this situation?" Typically, only a couple of hands would go up.

Then, I would launch into my story—the tale of a local kid, molested by his Scout leader, whose life falls apart in a vicious cycle of drugs and alcohol and just about every other addiction in the book, who commits an unspeakable act and ends up facing life in prison. The disaster that my life became—a procession of misery, torment, and murder—tends to set a new standard for how low one's life can sink. My audiences had to know that I knew, firsthand, the true desperation of utter defeat.

Still, I had come back. I was living proof that breaking the grip of addiction was possible. We talk about finding meaning and purpose in life. We talk about my work lobbying the legislature to change laws that allow predators to escape lawsuits, and about my fundraising for charities that serve victimized children.

My relief at escaping that old life, not to mention my joy and enthusiasm for doing good, must have shown through all those presentations, because when I got to the end of my remarks, I always asked the same two questions again:

"How many of you still feel defeated after hearing my story?" Nada! So far, not a single hand has ever been raised in response to that second inquiry.

"How many of you feel you can still achieve all your goals and dreams?" Everyone! I swear, it's always been unanimous. Every hand in the house goes up.

Audience appreciation is downright medicinal to me, a virtual drug that warms my heart and brightens my day and, most important, encourages me to keep sharing this story for as long as it makes a difference in the troubled life of anyone else.

Chapter Forty-Five

A FRIEND REQUEST

I was back in Trenton for the last round of hearings that we all hoped would lead, within a month or so, to a final vote on the Child Victims Act. The state senate Judiciary Committee convened in early March 2019 before a packed crowd that included sexual abuse victims and their families. Many held photos of their loved ones. I was one of more than three dozen witnesses set to testify.

It was clear from the opening gavel that emotions were running high. Even with a five-minute speaking limit on each witness, it figured to be a long session. And then the limit was routinely ignored: speakers had to be cut off by the chair, tempers flared, feelings were hurt, impatience soared. For the first time, I worried that we might be risking some of our broad support among the friendly, but frazzled, politicians.

When it was my turn, I tossed aside my script and gave the panel my minute-and-a-half version. I told them in bullet-point

concision how I was molested by my scoutmaster, a local sheriff's officer, and raped when I was twelve; how out of guilt and
shame I kept it a secret from my family and closest friends; how
it ruined my life, leading me to spiral into drug and alcohol addictions; how I had no option to seek damages and, as an adult,
took my Scout knife to my abuser's home and killed him. How no
one should follow in my footsteps.

I summed it up as I'd done before: "If you don't pass this
reform, there are sure to be more Clark Frederickses. And that
blood will be on your hands." No one could have delivered that
line with more authority than I did.

My warning was still fresh when the committee voted 8 to 1
to send the bill to the full senate. Then, in quick succession, the
assembly Judiciary Committee approved it as well, and the full
senate passed it with only one negative vote—32 to 1. Ten days
later, I was back in the capital to watch the final vote. The assembly made it unanimous, 71 to 0, sending the bill off to the
governor for his signature.

Those were heady days for all of us in the advocacy ranks. I
was proud of my contributions. At the same time, my speaking
schedule was packed. I addressed a prep school audience in the
Bronx. I shared my story in a talk-back session at New York City's
Off-Broadway Acorn Theatre after a performance of *Blackbird*, a
play about sex abuse.

I was booked to speak in the newly opened Sitnik Theatre at
Centenary University in Hackettstown, New Jersey. And I had
organized a charity event coming up in May that would benefit
three Newton-area community groups that supported victims of

sexual and domestic abuse. It was nearly a month away but the charity event had already sold out. A reporter from the *New Jersey Herald* had just interviewed me for a feature story about my new role as a motivational speaker.

Life was good. I was sober. I was fit and healthy. I was employed. I was doing good works. I was in demand to share my story. I had most of what I needed. Certainly, the broken man I had been—the guy who woke up every day angry or depressed or both—that guy was gone.

What I didn't have was someone to share my successes with, to be part of my new life. Of course, my mother was excited, delighted, and proud. But neither of us wanted to make a big deal about it in front of my brother, whose struggles only seemed to worsen as my successes multiplied.

Driving home alone from another late shift in the Boat House kitchen, I found myself fantasizing about the romance that got away—the college love that couldn't survive my fears of commitment and my screwed-up self-loathing. After all those years, the memory of an old love was still scratching the back of my brain. I was still kicking myself for losing the only person from my past that left another kind of hole in my heart—the whirlwind with the backpack that left me speechless in the Ell Center study hall at Northeastern when she landed with "Hi, my name is Lisa."

I knew a few things about Lisa Kaufman's life since we'd broken up almost thirty years ago. I was still in touch with my old college roommate Kevin, who married Lisa's college roommate, Anne Marie. They had told me that Lisa was married and had two sons, that she still lived in Westchester County, and that she had her own pediatric physical-therapy practice. Kevin and Ann Marie once showed me a picture of Lisa with her boys. I also knew that Ann Marie had kept Lisa informed about my arrest and when I got out of prison.

They knew that I still thought about Lisa, still wondered what she was doing and how things might have been if we'd stayed together. They knew because I told them. But only my mother had ever seen me break down sobbing tears of regret for letting her get away.

I had to assume that Lisa wasn't available romantically. After all, she never reached out after my release from prison. Her non-response was a response of sorts, or so I told myself. I could only have been something of a curiosity to her—but maybe that was enough. Maybe all I could do was move on and get on with getting over her.

There was a practical excuse, though, for us to have at least one more conversation. I was beginning to write about my life, writings that I thought might someday be read by others, and I felt that I needed permission to use her name in that account.

I tried to steel myself for whatever she might say—or maybe worse, what she might not say. *Why would Lisa ever want to hear from me again?* I imagined I was about to disrupt her white-picket-fence life like some unwelcome spring storm. Maybe all she'd say was *Leave me alone!* Well, at least that would be something.

Years of therapy had told me that as an abuse victim I was setting myself up for one of the worst possible situations—the psychological terror of vulnerability. I had spent most of my adult life avoiding it, but I was now finally resolved to face it. I had to make myself vulnerable to apologize for how I treated her, to get on with my life, and to know the truth, whatever that truth turned out to be.

So, I sent her a note on Facebook, extending a friend request "just to catch up and say hi." I told her that I had prayed for her over the years, hoping that she was having a wonderful life, and that the photos I'd seen of her and of her family suggested that everything was "going great, and I'm very happy for you."

After suggesting that we catch up sometime, "if you like," I gave her the short-form version of my life over the last three decades:

"I've been to the depths of hell on multiple occasions. I've experienced immense pain, torment, and heartache. And yet, I am the happiest and healthiest I've ever been in my life. I'm a motivational speaker and have three speeches in the next month. I'm an advocate and just played a role in getting a new child abuse bill passed in N.J. (something many said would never happen)."

As to my writing, I asked if she would mind if I mentioned her, at least by her first name. I signed off with "If you want to talk for a minute, here's my phone number."

I had written all of this. But I still hadn't sent it. As I contemplated it, I realized my hand was shaking. For the hundredth time, I asked myself, *Is this a good idea?*

What does it matter? I finally said to myself. *You've got to know one way or the other.*

And that settled it. I hit SEND. There was no turning back now.

Chapter Forty-Six

LOVE IS SAYING "SORRY"

Waiting for Lisa's response, I was like some kind of crack-head desperate to hear from my dope dealer. The time stamp on my outgoing Facebook message was precisely ten o'clock on a Monday morning. By lunchtime I'd made more than a dozen visits checking for her answer. And that was only the beginning. I went to bed that night still checking, still waiting. The fretting didn't end until the next evening—thirty-two hours and twenty-seven minutes later, according to my count.

It was worth the wait.

"Hi Clark, I am so happy to hear from you after all this time."

Yes! What a relief. It was Lisa's voice for sure. I could almost hear her.

She was in North Carolina with her youngest son on a college-scouting trip. That explained her delay. She also explained her early reluctance to reach out, back when she first learned about my crime and what had triggered it. She wrote:

"I was heartbroken about what you endured as a child . . . but I didn't know what to say to you. I have, however, thought about you often throughout my life and hoped you were healing and able to move forward. It sounds like you are doing some incredible and wonderful things with your life."

I was devouring every syllable. But I was especially struck by what she had to say about us. I don't think I breathed as I read, "Our times together so many years ago were both amazing and sad. I always knew something was holding you back from moving forward in our relationship. I now know that was true and letting me go was so selfless of you. It enabled me to move on and have a wonderful life."

She told me about her "two amazing sons" and her physical therapy practice, adding that I could definitely use her name in a book about my life. She closed with a nod to the future:

"Maybe when I get back from my trip [visiting colleges] we can find some time to talk."

Her only reference to a husband or a life of love and romance was a brief description: "I am married to a good man." Remembering Lisa and her typically enthusiastic displays of friendship and affection, it sounded like faint praise. Or perhaps I was just seeing what I wanted to see. I had to be patient until she got home and we could find some time to talk—preferably in person.

"Oh, Lisa, you made my day," I wrote. I attached a link to the local newspaper that had published a front-page feature that morning about my motivational speaking tour, headlined "Fredericks, Who Killed Alleged Abuser in Stillwater, Telling His Story."

Mostly, I hoped to put Lisa at ease about keeping in touch: "I would love to talk when you're back. I didn't know if you would think I was disrupting your life. . . . Whew, thankfully that wasn't the case. I am putting myself out to the world and being as transparent as I can be about everything in my life, past and present. . . . Yes, I let you go, and I regretted it every day. But I also knew I could never have been what you needed and deserved at the time."

Harboring too much pain and secrecy in those days, I tried to explain, made the intimacy of marriage "an impossibility."

One week later, she reappeared in my Facebook messenger thanking me for that newspaper story and saying that she was "looking forward to connecting soon." By that time, I had just addressed my first general audience—not a group of inmates or recovering addicts who *had* to listen to me, not a captive bunch, but a gathering of students and private citizens at Centenary University that came specifically to hear my story.

In my message, I told Lisa what I had talked about to that crowd, about "how the pain and secrecy I carried caused me to sabotage and ruin the one true love in my life. I told them I've never felt such passion and love since. The Universe matched these two perfect people together and I destroyed it, and it's pained me ever since.

"I'm not trying to get you all emotional, Lisa. I just want you to know that I know I failed us, and how sorry I am. I'm not trying to mess with the harmony of your current life. I'm just addressing my failures and regrets from thirty years ago."

Our Facebook conversations went on for more than a week.

We talked about what we had been doing in recent years. She was surprised that I worked as a chef. "When did you learn to cook?"

Yeah, what else did we not know about each other thirty years later?

During many hours of computer messaging, I must have found a couple hundred different ways to tell Lisa over and over how sorry I was for walking away from her. I couldn't stop, even after she told me to "stop apologizing" and insisted that what I gave her was actually a gift—"a chance at the type of life you couldn't give me."

She wrote, "I made a choice when I thought you had moved on that led to having my sons and being with someone who was devoted to me—and who was here for me. I went on with my life and all that came with it . . . but to be completely honest . . . I never forgot you or our crazy, spontaneous moments together."

Our time trading messages had turned into a sort of unmediated couple's therapy. It seemed to me that we were both still crazy about the people we used to be thirty years ago. Now we were simply exploring an old friendship. I thought we should come out from behind our keyboards and meet somewhere. Lisa was open to it—so long as it was in broad daylight and at a public place.

We picked the next Monday morning. We both had the day off and chose to meet at a Starbucks midway between our homes in Sussex and Westchester Counties.

That's how we ended up a couple of days later on State Route 17 in Mahwah, New Jersey. I couldn't speak for Lisa, but I felt, in the days before our meeting, a powerful sense of hope, like maybe I had just stepped into the pages of my very own romance novel.

REMAINS OF A PAST

What Lisa never mentioned through those days of catching up online was anything directly related to the state of her marriage. I didn't know, for instance, that she and her husband had been in and out of marriage counseling over the years, that they were little more than roommates, and that she was already considering a legal separation, once their youngest went off to college. Even as I wrote to her that I didn't want to "disrupt your white picket fence life," she was telling me that she just wanted to be friends. So, as excited as I was to see Lisa—and to throw my arms around her—I was still trying to check my enthusiasm and my expectations.

Approaching the Mahwah Starbucks, I saw her. It was as if thirty years had never happened. Lisa was standing next to her car looking exactly like she did the last time I saw her. I wheeled quickly into the parking spot next to her, scrambling to get out of my seat belt and out of my car. In another moment she was in my arms . . . and I was kissing her . . . and she was pushing me away.

"Whoa! Whoa! Whoa!"

Well, so much for my checked enthusiasm. I could have apologized, again, but I didn't. Not this time, not on what had to be about the happiest moment in my whole life. Lisa started for the Starbucks front door, but I stopped her. I had left something in my car. I retrieved my briefcase.

Neither of us was in a hurry to get into the line for lattes. I found a seat on a low wall just outside the shop's entrance. The ledge put six-foot-three me eye to eye with five-foot-four her. It was perfect. All I wanted to do was look at her. I felt like the oldest living teenager. We sat there only a few minutes before Lisa looked out across the parking lot and seemed suddenly alarmed.

"Clark, why are you parked in a handicapped space?"

I hadn't noticed anything but Lisa when pulling into that spot. I jumped up, left my briefcase in her care, and hurried over to move my car. Coming back, I could see she was giving my briefcase a hard look.

"You take a briefcase on all your dates?" she joked.

"Is that what this is? A date?"

Light banter with Lisa had always been a treat. It was just another reason to savor this blast from the past. Eventually, we moved inside, ordered our drinks, and took a table. That's when I opened the briefcase.

"What have you got in there?" she said, feigning suspicion.

"See for yourself." I turned the open case for her to see a loose collection of mail, including cards, letters, and stamped envelopes.

One had her return address. All of them were in Lisa's handwriting.

"What is this?"

"They're all yours."

"I know! But, Clark—what is this?"

I didn't really have to tell her. She knew immediately. It was every card and letter Lisa had ever written to me—right up to and including the last one, the one she signed off, "I hope we will always be friends."

She sat there stunned into silence, if only for the moment, leafing through the assortment of love letters she had written. The collection amounted to the archival remains of our old romance. For more than twenty years, this accumulated literary treasure occupied the special top drawer of my bedroom dresser.

Police left them strewn on that bedroom floor after a thorough search of my personal belongings on the afternoon of my arrest. My mother had picked up the mess left by the forensics team and, recognizing what the letters represented to me, stashed them under her bed for safekeeping—until I came home and reclaimed them.

All I hoped for now, over our coffees and love letters in Mahwah, was that Lisa would understand the truth: That when we split up, it wasn't because I didn't love her. I did then. I always had. And I still did.

I shared that very private fact with Howie Ryan about a week later, confiding that after my first meeting with Lisa I knew that I was in love again, or still, or whatever. My arresting officer's advice worked out well the last time when he told me to keep my mouth shut until I had a lawyer. His advice about Lisa was just as direct:

"By no means ever let her get away again."

Chapter Forty-Eight

BEGINNINGS AND ENDS

My brother Jay's decline was a slow-motion train wreck that haunts me to this day. Our lives began as mirror images of each other—two boys raised in the same household, by the same parents, during the same era, with similar advantages and disadvantages, abused by the same family friend and pedophile predator.

I floundered as a young man, trapped in my addictions, before finding escape from my victimhood through self-discipline, prayer, and meditation—by way of prison and some lifesaving psychological counseling. *Thank you very much, State of New Jersey.*

Jay thrived as a young man—becoming a successful business-man and family man and respected member of his community—while also keeping his childhood traumas buried deep inside, telling no one and avoiding even thinking about it himself. That is, until his kid brother's very public actions turned a spotlight on the unresolved issues still lurking in the shadows of his big brother's private life.

Neither of us would ever be the same. He disappeared into some of the addictions I had just escaped—turning our lives into reverse images in the same mirror. I use a metaphor from Psalms 23 to compare my early struggles with Jay's later troubles. That's the verse about walking through the valley of the shadow of death. I was in that valley for a long time. I mean, I stopped walking, pitched a tent, and set up camp. Although it was much easier said than done, I had learned that the key was to *keep* walking, to get through those shadows, to keep moving.

Jay stopped moving ahead one day in February 2023. I found him facedown and unresponsive on the floor of our mother's kitchen. After calling an ambulance, I tried to resuscitate him, pleading for him to hang on and fight back. But he was gone before anyone else got there. Of all the people I was able to help, of all the fans who credited me for inspiring their recovery efforts, the one who mattered most, the one that I could never reach, was the big brother who had always looked out for me.

He had been so much more successful than I was at hiding the secrets and denying the guilt and shame that came with it. How terribly ironic that the unlikely string of events that would save me would destroy him. Facing the truth had set me free. It broke Jay, who wasn't ready to face that himself.

He had tried to clean up and kick his alcohol habit. He was sober for about eight months the year before he died. But Jay never kicked his anger, an anger I knew only too well. Getting sober was never going to be enough. Getting over that rage was an essential first step to getting past being the victim.

What I tell people is *You've got to start your day off with wins. Get up early, eat a good breakfast; pray, meditate, do yoga, work out; read something inspirational, have a mantra of your own, repeat it daily; make your bed— because getting started right sets a tone for the day. Repetition makes it all a habit. And all that self-discipline builds and keeps renewing emotional muscle.*

I could never convince my brother. If anything, my very public downfall and celebrated recovery seemed to be more of a burden to him. He called me "the golden boy," and it wasn't a compliment. And the last person he wanted preaching at him was his younger brother.

Ultimately, the deadly combination of alcoholism and diabetes brought him down at the age of sixty-three. At his funeral I pointed out that Jay had followed my lead in one way—working out at the gym with our friend Robin, the owner. "Even on that last day of his life he was at the gym," I told my fellow mourners. "It gives me some solace knowing that he hadn't given up on himself. He was still trying; even though he was self-destructing, there was still a sign of hope in there."

After Jay's passing, my mother decided to let go of the family house she had continued to live in so that my brother had a place to sleep that wasn't his pickup truck. Soon after the funeral, she put down a deposit on a lovely senior citizen residence in our area, and we started to prep the house for the real estate market.

By this point in 2023, Lisa had been separated and divorced for nearly three years. We were spending a lot of time together, but I had continued to live in our family house helping my now ninety-three-year-old mother deal with household maintenance, meals, and paying the bills. And, while Jay was there, taking care of my heavy-drinking, too-often fall-down-drunk brother.

After Jay died, Mom needed time to deal with such a tough loss. There was no rush. It would take time to fix up and sell the house and to arrange for Mom's move.

Lisa and I were dating across state lines in all that time, anticipating a life together. As much as we were eager to get on with that, no one wanted it to come faster than my mother did. She kept apologizing that she was standing in the way of true love.

When the stars were finally aligned, Mom headed off to her new home without looking back. I knew I'd have to stay with the house until it sold, but Lisa and I dared to contemplate a new beginning for ourselves after all these years. Like me, she still remembered our first encounter in the study hall at Northeastern University.

"You know," she said, "it's only been thirty-seven years since we met each other."

Only? I detected a smart-ass remark coming.

"What do you think?" she said, trying not to break into a big grin. "Now, can we finally live together?"

What could I say but:

"Lisa, my love, why are you always trying to rush me?"

FINALE

During the summer of 2023, I was invited to deliver the keynote address at a New Jersey State Police crime lab conference. This midday event coincided with an anniversary: one of the worst days in my life. I was standing before a state police crowd on precisely the day and at the very hour that eleven years earlier state police were surrounding my house to arrest me.

So, for this speaking engagement, I tweaked my standard presentation. After sharing basic background stories of my abuse and how I had dealt with my abuser, I looked out into that law enforcement audience of 150 forensics detectives and teasingly deadpanned, "Because you did your jobs correctly, I had to spend five long years in prison."

Unsure whether I was being funny, my audience held its breath for a couple seconds—until I grinned and assured them, "And I really can't thank you enough."

I explained how prison counseling had helped me heal and turn my life around. "What you did saved me. Because you did your jobs and sent me to prison, I was able to get clean and sober. Because you did your jobs and sent me to prison, I took my life in a new direction and became an advocate helping to reform the state's statute of limitations law for child sex abuse victims. And because you did your jobs and I healed, I finally reached out to the college sweetheart I'd walked away from thirty years before. Now we've reunited and started our lives together."

I gestured to Lisa in the front row. She gave a little wave, and the crowd cheered. A moment later the cheers swelled into an eruption. Everyone in the crowd was on their feet. Eleven years nearly to the hour after a team of their colleagues had swarmed my home to arrest me for murder, these 150 New Jersey state police employees were giving me a standing ovation.

ACKNOWLEDGMENTS

First and foremost, to William C. Rempel—a bestselling author and award-winning investigative journalist for the *Los Angeles Times* for thirty-six years. Bill and I worked together for over two years as I described one scene of my life after another. He visited my hometown and interviewed all the key players that were a part of my journey. Bill was able to take the harrowing material that was my life and articulate it with eloquent simplicity. There are not enough words to show my appreciation for his work as both collaborator and editor.

David Halpern, at David Halpern Literary Management. My immense thanks for representation as my literary agent. We've been at this together since 2017 through both smooth and rocky roads. To think that we will finally see this in print is an extremely gratifying moment for both of us. Thank you for believing in my story and the need for it to be told.

Amar Deol, who acquired the book initially at Atria. Thank you for seeing the impact my journey could have on society. You realized the significance of this topic early on and I am grateful.

Yaniv Soha, my current editor at Atria Publishing Group. You read the first draft and were instantly all-in with your commitment. I appreciate you getting behind my work 100 percent. Thank you for your keen editorial eye in fine-tuning the material.

To Hannah Frankel and everyone else at Atria and Simon & Schuster. Thank you for all the behind-the-scenes work and for always being ready to help and lend support.

To my mother and other family members. Thank you for your unwavering support through some extremely trying times. You all helped me to get through the darkest point in my life. Without your love, I may not have made it through.

Dan Perez, the best defense attorney bar none. You had both compassion and strength. You gave me hope when I just wanted to wallow in despair. Thank you for my freedom.

Finally, to best supporting actress in a nonfiction memoir. From college sweethearts to modern-day lovers. You were able to accept all the dark ugliness of my past and see the man with unlimited potential that you had originally fallen in love with. Thank you, Lisa, for allowing our love to flourish.

ABOUT THE AUTHOR

Clark **Fredericks's** story has inspired major reform of the statutes that once severely limited the rights of child abuse victims to sue their abusers. His story has been featured by *CBS News*, *ABC News*, *Fox News*, *People*, the *Los Angeles Times*, *Daily Mail*, and more. Fredericks is a popular motivational speaker, and he remains an outspoken victims' rights advocate. He lives in Northern New Jersey.